Agnes Law

Eyes so blue

Vol. III

Agnes Law

Eyes so blue
Vol. III

ISBN/EAN: 9783337052119

Printed in Europe, USA, Canada, Australia, Japan

Cover: Foto ©ninafisch / pixelio.de

More available books at **www.hansebooks.com**

EYES SO BLUE.

A Novel.

BY

AGNES LAW.

IN THREE VOLUMES.
VOL. III.

London:
SAMUEL TINSLEY & CO.,
10 SOUTHAMPTON STREET, STRAND.
1878.
All rights reserved.]

CONTENTS OF VOL. III.

CHAP.		PAGE
I.	Suspicions Aroused	1
II.	Confession	26
III.	New Hopes for Ivor	44
IV.	Stricken with Grief	62
V.	Seen from the Street	79
VI.	Vacillation	99
VII.	He cometh not, She said	128
VIII.	On the Beach	138
IX.	Dolores	162
X.	Don't forget Me	182
XI.	A Friend in Need	207
XII.	Once again	229
XIII.	Parting	253
XIV.	Reconciliation	265

EYES SO BLUE.

CHAPTER I.

SUSPICIONS AROUSED.

> O'er all the landscape far and near
> High noon its glamour throws,
> Kind fancy calls my lost ones here,
> Fond memory backward goes.
>   REV. J. TROUTBECK, M.A.

"IT is all very well for you to talk of forgiveness, Monticth, but there are some injuries that it is impossible either to forget or forgive. Why should I not learn the whole truth of my brother's treachery? Surely it is more than human nature is capable of, to remain passive after such trials as I have had to endure!"

Lord Durant spoke excitedly—nay, almost

irritably; he was walking backwards and forwards, up and down the room, trying to repress the angry, revengeful feelings towards his brother that were surging in his heart.

"I certainly did not mean to give offence, my lord; I merely suggested that perhaps the past had better be buried in oblivion," answered Claude Montieth. "The facts of Major Durant's wrong-doing are known to you; is it any use inquiring into the details? An interview with Sister Veronica must necessarily be painful both to you and her."

"Painful or not, it must be undergone," said the nobleman, firmly; and then, lowering his voice, he asked in a hurried whisper, "Surely you are not afraid—for me—that these heavy troubles may prove too much. Ah, I sometimes almost hope it could be so! Perhaps even the oblivion of madness would be better, happier, than the misery of acute consciousness."

Poor Lord Durant! From the bottom of his heart Claude pitied him, as he watched the look of unalterable sorrow that seemed to be even past the desire for sympathy.

For a few minutes they both remained in a silence that spoke more deeply than words. Some days had elapsed since Mavis's disappearance—days of futile hope and expectancy, that kind of uncertainty that is worse to bear than full confirmation of the most terrible fears.

Lord Durant would go on hoping: his Mavis, his lovely little wife, surely could not be gone from him for ever: and then afterwards came the crushing sorrow, the end of doubt and suspense, and he knew it was all over; even the heart that had to the last refused belief in that which others felt a certainty, was obliged to own that Mavis was dead to him—worse than dead, he kept saying over and over again, stolen from him by the brother he had once loved and trusted. How incomprehensible *that* love and trust seemed to him now that it was only with feelings amounting to hatred that he could think of Lionel.

And to escape from the torture of recollections that were becoming insupportable he had sought companionship and fled away from the luxurious apartments in the hotel, where everything reminded him of Mavis, to the bare, dismal attic that Sybil and Claude Montieth called home. He envied them even their poverty; for to his eyes it seemed full of sweet content, the happiness that true love alone could bring. His heart was touched by the kindly welcome and simple hospitality, as well as the true innate delicacy by which all mention of his harrowing sorrow was avoided by the three who now seemed to him the only friends he had left.

Although he had differed from Claude, the suggestion that Sister Veronica (who was lawfully his wife, and by no crime of her own, but by the falsehood and deception of others, had been cruelly wronged) might be longing for an explanation did not leave his mind. He pondered over it until he came to the same conclusion, that, painful as the ordeal would be to him, he had no right to refuse a meeting.

Sybil readily volunteered to go to the convent. She had been anxious to see Sister Veronica; but without a positive errand had thought that a visit might at that time be considered an intrusion. She had no difficulty in gaining an admittance into the building, as she was already known by sight there, and only had a few moments to wait before Sister Veronica entered, calm and stately as ever, with no change on her serene countenance, save that it was a trifle paler than before.

"I know what you wish to tell me," she said, with her usual placid manner, that to Sybil's eyes bespoke heartlessness. "The news of Lionel Durant's elopement has become known even in this quiet retreat. I am not surprised. I knew him to be like his mother—crafty, treacherous, innately wicked; who but a villain could have acted thus? I could see how Gerald Durant loved that little creature; he must have believed her really to be his wife, for he is a good man. If I had behaved to him as I ought, this sorrow would never have overtaken him, and my life would not have been one long season of unavailing repentance."

"But surely Lord Durant was to blame—

about you, I mean," stammered Sybil, suddenly growing confused, for she felt she was touching on a delicate subject, especially when she noticed a spasm of pain cross Sister Veronica's face, one of the only signs of feeling she had ever betrayed in her presence.

"Perhaps he may have been, I do not know; it is not for me to judge,—I must only think of my own faults. I never cared for him as a wife should: I was cold, hard, indifferent. I must have been blind then. I had chosen my destiny. I should have done my best to act rightly. But enough of this: I have long buried the past away from my thoughts."

"Lord Durant sent me to know if you will grant him an interview; it would be a satisfaction to learn the truth of the treachery with which you both have been deceived," said Sybil. "Will you consent to a meeting? If you would rather not do so, I am sure he will give it up."

A change came over the rather severe countenance, making it look sterner than ever.

"He has a right to know all. Why should I shrink from revealing the wrongs that have been perpetrated?" she replied, quietly. "You can go back and tell Gerald Durant to appoint a time and place of meeting. I have no time to say any more; my duties call me away."

"Has she grown colder and harder?" Sybil asked herself, and the tears sprang to her eyes, when she thought of Sister Veronica's cool, collected manner. "She might surely show some emotion after knowing that her husband, whom she had so long believed dead, is alive! Can she have a heart? Surely it cannot be, or she could never have behaved cruelly to kind, good Lord Durant."

"Cannot you come with me now?" she continued, speaking aloud. "I should think it will be better to get the interview over."

Sister Veronica hesitated a moment.

"It must be, I suppose," she said. "It may as well come now. Yes, I will go with you."

She led the way without a word, and

walked on first, with a firm, stately tread, pausing when she arrived at the stairs that led to Claude's studio, waiting for Sybil to come up, and together they went into the presence of Lord Durant. He had not expected the return so soon, and during his conversation with Claude he did not hear that any one had entered the room until Sybil's voice said,—

"Sister Veronica is here, Lord Durant."

They all looked up quickly. Ivor raised his eyes from the water-colour sketch over which he was busied, and Claude attempted to rise from his sofa, near to which the nobleman was seated.

She came in swiftly, the colour deepening on her cheeks for a second, but only Sybil could see how she was trembling.

"Do not go; all of you please to stay: all that I have to communicate to Lord Durant will be better said before witnesses," she began, raising her calm and still beautiful eyes towards Claude, and noticing the extra hue of pallor on his face; for even during this trying meeting her quick comprehensive glance did not fail to take note of the increasing delicacy so plainly indicated. Lord Durant advanced towards her; one steady, searching look into his face, and then her eyes were cast down. He was the first to speak.

"Agatha," he began, and his voice was tremulous with deep emotion, which was such a striking contrast to her coolness, "I want to know the truth. Why was I led to believe that you were dead? Speak! Tell me, had you any share in this dreadful deception?"

"Hush, Lord Durant,—remember what you are saying!" exclaimed Sister Veronica, her voice raised above its ordinary pitch. "Did you ever know me practise deception? did I ever by word or look say anything but the truth to you—you who once deceived me? Ah! you may forget, but I do not; never shall I to my dying day be able to blot from my memory that awful moment, when I knew that I was the wife of a madman."

Lord Durant visibly recoiled and staggered back, as if struck a heavy blow.

"Agatha, do not be cruel,—do not add to my trials," he exclaimed, in a hoarse whisper. "I ought not to have doubted you; but, tell me, was it Lionel's doing?"

"I suppose so," she answered, coldly and sarcastically. "Surely during the last few days you might have possessed sufficient penetration to discover both the originator of all the underhand dealing, and the motives that prompted him. Are the Durant estates so very worthless that such people as Lionel Durant or his mother should shrink from committing a crime in order to possess them? Was it not easy to deceive me? Why should I have any reason to disbelieve Lady Durant when she told me you had died in the asylum to which I knew you had been taken?"

"I see it all! I understand it now!" cried Lord Durant. "From first to last it has been one long system of plotting against me. I remember now as clearly as I believed it then—the time when Lionel brought me the news of yours and your child's death. He said it had happened in Naples. But what has become of him—the child, my baby boy—whom I was permitted to see, and just for one moment to hold in my arms? They yielded to my entreaties, and brought him, but they doubted me; they were afraid even of trusting my son with me then, as if I could have harmed him, an innocent babe! No, thank God! I never was so mad as they believed me to be. But, tell me, does he still live?—was the news of his death also a falsehood?"

"No, Lord Durant; I should have thought you knew my child never lived,—it died at its birth," replied Sister Veronica, as calmly as ever. "The facts are plain enough to both of us now. Lady Durant and her son —who, I conclude, was at that time merely a tool in her hands—successfully accomplished the separation that appears to have been their aim."

She turned away with as much coolness and indifference as if she had been engaged in a mere common-place discussion which she considered ended. The nobleman was silent for a moment, striving to arrange in order the strange medley of thoughts and recollections that were crowding into his mind. Sybil, who had been an interested auditor, now advanced, and laid her hand on Sister Veronica's arm.

"Did not you hear what Lord Durant stated just now?" she said; "it appears like a further complication in this mystery. You have spoken of your child's death, whilst Lord Durant mentions having afterwards seen it alive and well."

Sybil said no more, but her face expressed the horror that was reflected in the minds of all present. Lord Durant was the first to break silence.

"Surely Lionel cannot have done this also! Can he have committed such a crime? Is it possible that he murdered the child!" he said, not passionately, but with the low utterance of one who scarcely dared to breathe such a fearful suspicion.

The protracted, intense stillness that fell on all in the room served to prove that there were none there to whose minds that suspicion appeared unfounded. Sister Veronica alone shook her head. "No!" she said, resolutely, "it cannot be: probably it was a mental delusion. Lord Durant never beheld his son."

All this time Ivor had remained quiet, still apparently employed over his drawing; but he was intently listening to the strange, romantic story, one that sounded almost like a fiction from its improbability; but interwoven with it, mingling like some dream of the past, came indistinct reminiscences of words casually uttered, maybe thoughts of childhood, of his old grandfather's tales about his mother's time of service at Pen Vychan Castle—that mother who had never seemed to care for him, but, as soon as he could walk alone, had given him up to the old man who had filled the place of both parents to him.

He had been told that he was born the same day as the young heir to the Durant estates, the baby whose life had been so short. The old man had even once or twice uttered a wish that their positions had been reversed; that the widow's child, who had been so little comfort to his mother, had died, and Lord Durant's child had lived instead.

In his days of childhood he had often spoken about that baby, picturing to himself what its life would have been had it lived. And now, recalling old times, he distinctly remembered how his mother had rebuked him, and ridiculed his foolish day-dreams, as she called them. And when he heard Lord Durant's exclamation of horror, many long-forgotten incidents and chance words that he had heard and partially forgotten, rushed back into his memory. He felt Sister Veronica's eyes fixed on him with a searching, scrutinizing gaze.

"Ivor Morgan," she said, slowly, "can it be—is it possible that you are the son of my servant, Jane Morgan, whose child was born the same day as mine?"

"Yes, that was my mother's name," replied Ivor. "She was Lady Durant's maid; my father was drowned at sea. I was the child who was born at Pen Vychan Castle."

He uttered these words carelessly, merely

as a reply to the question put to him, never thinking that they would affect the whole course of his life; but, brief as the sentence was, it shed a ray of light into Sister Veronica's brain.

"Probably it was no delusion," she said: "no doubt you were the child that was shown to Lord Durant, and they made him believe you were his son."

All this time Lord Durant sat with his face hidden in his hands. He heard the conversation that was going on; at other times it would have aroused his interest, but now he felt too utterly miserable to give more than a passing thought to his dead child. It had happened so long ago—nearly eighteen years—and he had almost, until now, forgotten that Mervyn had once had an elder brother.

But Ivor's words roused him. "Born the same day," it seemed strange that the tiny infant, whose face he was able distinctly to recall to his mind, would, had he lived, have been nearly a man, the same age as the tall, handsome-looking youth who during these last days of trouble had shown him so much sympathy.

The nobleman looked up suddenly; his eager glance met Ivor's, and all at once there came an overpowering thought, one that for a second made his heart beat quicker with dawning hope.

With an exclamation of surprise, Claude sprang from his sofa with more vigour than seemed possible with his feeble looks. He had been quietly regarding both Lord Durant and Ivor; and when the latter had spoken, something in his look and manner had caused the look of astonishment. But he checked himself hastily. "It cannot be," he said; "better to let it rest than raise hopes that most probably will be futile."

Sister Veronica came forward. "Lord Durant, it is time I returned to the convent, to the life that I have chosen, and in which I hope to end my days. We are both satisfied now. I intend to take no further steps in the matter, but leave you to deal with Lady Durant and her equally wicked son as you think best. It is you they have wronged most deeply. I bear them no particular malice; they told me you were dead, and you were dead to me — what did it matter? Your conduct in deceiving me about your former insanity was sufficient to justify my conduct in retiring into the haven where I have found rest; and I believe by this time I have fully atoned for any wrong I have done to you. You will not see me again; any further communication you may wish can be done by writing. Good-bye."

"Stay a minute, Agatha; do not go yet!" exclaimed Lord Durant.

She hesitated, and turned back with her hand on the door. "What do you wish to say?" she asked, surprised at his visible agitation. His naturally kind heart rebelled fiercely against this cold parting with her who, although all affection appeared to have gone, was legally his wife.

"Say you forgive me, Agatha?" he asked. I know I did wrong; but I was young, and oh, the horror I felt at making the revelation!"

The pain expressed in his voice seemed

to touch her. "Yes, Gerald," she answered, more gently than she had before spoken. We have both much to forgive; it is all over now. Once more, farewell.

In a moment she was gone. She had vanished from his sight as quietly as she had come, leaving her husband standing motionless, bewildered by the varied emotions that the interview had produced.

Ivor's thoughts were also very painful. He loved Sister Veronica with a kind of worshipping reverence, regarding her as one far above him in every respect. Good, wise, and tender, she had been so gentle and sympathizing, coming, as she did, at the time when he felt so utterly lonely, with his suffering friend; and now she was so changed, so cold and indifferent, that it produced a deep pain in his heart. "She cannot altogether lack feeling," he thought; "it is impossible to believe it. And how she could behold Lord Durant's sad face and not pity him, passes my comprehension." At length he spoke. "You should not think harshly of her, my lord," he said, unable to resist the impulse to plead her cause. "She is a truly good lady! Oh, I wish you could have seen and known her as she really is!"

Lord Durant looked at him with astonishment. "Surely I ought to know her better than you," he answered, with a sad, bitter smile. "I try to think of her as leniently as I can, but she is hard hearted and unforgiving."

Surely these words did not come from the lips of Lord Durant, whom Ivor had always regarded as his ideal of all that was true, noble, and withal so gentle and inexpressibly kind—Jessie's friend, whom she had often said she loved almost next to her parents.

"No, you do not really know her true character as she is now," Ivor replied, boldly, feeling bound to defend his good friend. "I do not know what she was in times gone by, but now her life is spent in works of goodness; she tries to crush her natural feelings and emotions. That cold manner is, I am certain, assumed to hide her real nature."

He turned away in silence, fearing lest his words might have displeased his patron.

But, no; Lord Durant was still looking at him with a strange earnestness—almost a longing, hopeful expression. Once or twice he appeared about to speak, but, hastily checking the impulse, he rose and left the room.

"Sybil," said Claude, calling his wife to his sofa, as they were alone later on in the day, after Ivor had set out for his daily visit to Donato's studio, "a curious idea came into my mind during Sister Veronica's visit. I cannot tell if it is more than a fancy, but for a moment I imagined it: stranger things have happened. Can it be possible that Ivor is Lord Durant's son; that the two babies were changed by that designing woman, the dowager Lady Durant? The likeness is extraordinary in the lad to most of the Durants; I can even trace a resemblance to Sister Veronica, especially when his face is in repose."

Sybil looked at her husband in silent surprise; she shook her head. "I do not think it can be so," she said, presently, "it is so improbable; besides, it sounds too good to be true. I cannot imagine any better fortune happening to Ivor than that he could be proved to be Lord Durant's heir. I only wish it was possible; but I fear it is imagination arising from partiality and gratitude to Ivor."

"I think it is more than mere fancy," answered Claude. "I do not like to raise Lord Durant's hopes, but I confess I should like to mention my suspicions to him. It is hardly probable that, as he evidently suspected, the child was murdered. Wicked as she is, his stepmother would scarcely dare to commit such a horrible crime, even to secure her own son's inheritance, which, of course, is the motive of all her deception."

"Raise Lord Durant's hopes!" repeated his wife; "I should hardly think it would do so. To him Ivor is but a mere fisherman, or at best a poor obscure artist, with scarcely any education. Of course he does not see his real worth—how thoroughly good and clever he is."

"But, Sybil," interrupted Claude, "remember that at present Major Durant is his brother's heir: after what has happened, I should think he would be glad to find that his son still lived, and that the estates would pass to an honest, upright man, even if he did not possess the outward semblance of a gentleman."

Ivor's entrance of course put an end to the conversation; but Sybil's natural love of romance was roused. Little by little she tried to put together all she had seen or heard, until it gradually began to assume a clearer shape in her eyes, and, after a time, did not seem so very impossible. She knew most of the particulars of Lord Durant's history; living for so long in St. Hilda's, surrounded by so much to remind her of the old family, she had inquired about the living members of it, and partly from various sources, and also from Mavis, she had learnt the greater part of the history of Lord Durant's younger days. And Ivor had also often spoken about himself, and of his recollections of Pen Vychan, even of his love for Jessie Williams, to which he had never alluded to any one else.

Everything seemed to tend to the same conclusion; even the well-known fact of Mrs. Hughes's want of affection for Ivor appeared a strong link in the chain of evidence.

And all the evening as they sat together—for Lord Durant preferred to spend much of his time with his friends—she noticed how attentively the nobleman was regarding the young man; watching each movement, each expression and look, of the face that had once or twice caused him to start with surprise, as if struck by the strange likeness to—whom, he had never before paused to inquire.

"Did Lord Durant suspect anything?" Sybil asked herself, as whenever she looked up from her sewing she noticed a brighter look on the nobleman's face; not much change, but a slight relaxation from the settled melancholy expression.

From that time Claude's health began to show signs of improvement, and soon he was able to take some interest in his painting. It was not much that he could do, he was still so very weak, but even the slight indications of slowly returning health were sufficient to rouse Sybil from the state of despondency into which the near approach of poverty had thrown her.

She sometimes wished that Lord Durant's mind was not so entirely occupied with his own misery; perhaps then he might have noticed how poor they were, and given them some help: she felt inclined to blame him as selfish, and even once hinted so to her husband.

"Poor Lord Durant!" Claude replied. "We cannot wonder, with his own troubles, that he does not notice the wants of those round him. We must wait and hope a little longer; if I can only find a purchaser for my present works we shall get on."

He alluded to half a dozen small watercolour drawings that he had nearly completed. They were all he could accomplish; and even to Sybil's eyes they appeared poor and commonplace, in contrast to the style in which he had painted before his illness.

But no sooner were they finished than they

were sold ; Louis Hamilton was the purchaser. He had, he stated, bought them for a gentleman who wished his name to remain a secret. Although this was all he revealed, neither Claude nor Sybil could be deceived as to the identity of the purchaser, and they appreciated the kind instinct that had prompted Lord Durant to help them thus, and only regretted that the manner in which he had done so, prevented the possibility of expressing the gratitude they felt.

CHAPTER II.

CONFESSION.

> I do forgive thee,
> Unnatural though thou art!
> SHAKSPEARE.

The bright light of day seldom penetrated into the gloomy drawing-room at the Deanery of St. Hilda's. Although the summer sun was shining brightly outside, the dense overgrown mass of evergreens effectually excluded its beams from the low, narrow windows with their heavy drapery. On one of the darkest, gloomiest sides of the room sat Mrs. Melcombe and the dowager Lady Durant; the latter was leaning back in an easy-chair, her hands crossed idly on her lap, and a look of care and sadness on her face. She was considerably aged in appearance; there were more white threads amongst her still-abundant hair; the light in her eyes was dimmed, and there was a peculiar weariness and listlessness in each movement that plainly indicated that she had gone through some heavy trouble.

The shock produced by the news of her son's disappearance with Mavis had for a time almost robbed her of reason. It was in Lionel's welfare that all the hopes of her life had been centred. It was almost more than a mother's love that had prompted her in all her actions, that even led her to commit crimes, to practise deception for so many years for his sake, and now he had disgraced his name and brought upon it publicity and scandal that tore her heart to contemplate.

How she had been told she did not know; the fact seemed too horrible to be thought of; she only realized that in the height of the London season the name of Lionel Durant would be talked of everywhere. And so to escape from the haunts of society she accepted Mrs. Melcombe's warmly expressed invitation to go to St. Hilda's, and in the quiet of the cathedral city she was able to grow calmer, and her hostess's kind, sympathizing manner soothed her troubles, for Mrs. Melcombe could be both gentle and sympathetic when it served her own purpose.

They had been talking about the topic that was uppermost in the minds of both ladies. It was a relief to Lady Durant to try and find excuses for her son's conduct, and there was nobody to whom she felt she could talk so freely as to Mrs. Melcombe, for the friendship that had commenced on the day of little Mervyn's christening, had, during the time the dean's family had spent in London, ripened into intimacy.

"You know I never had a very good opinion of that frivolous little woman," said Mrs. Melcombe. "I believe that it was partly her influence that induced Sybil to disgrace herself as she did; they were far too friendly. The longer I live the more certain I am that the less you have to do with such low kind of people as she must have been, the better. A little actress! I am sure Lord Durant ought to have been ashamed of himself; at his age he should have known better than exalt a young person like that out of her proper rank; however, I am sure I am excessively sorry for Lord Durant, he appeared to care for her far more than she deserved."

An angry frown darkened Lady Durant's face.

"It is I who am to blame!" she exclaimed, fiercely. "I first brought her into Pen Vychan Castle, never dreaming that she would entrap Lord Durant into marrying her. I was foolish enough to be deceived by her pretty face and assumed innocence; she must have known the power of beauty."

As she uttered these words Isabel Ingram entered; there was a subdued, quiet sadness about her that plainly showed how deeply she resented the disgrace of her sister's marriage; but now there was a look which, with the increased paleness on her cheeks, showed that she was visibly agitated. She advanced towards Lady Durant.

"There is a visitor for you in the library," she said; "it is Lord Durant: he wishes to speak to you."

"Lord Durant? What! has he returned?" exclaimed Mrs. Melcombe, whose loud voice overpowered an involuntary cry of surprise that had risen to her friend's lips.

"Yes; he says he arrived in England this morning," answered Isabel. "It quite startled me when he was shown into the library. I inquired after Sybil, but he never replied; he seemed scarcely aware of my question, and is so strange and preoccupied in manner."

Lady Durant rose hastily, and, with a firmer step than usual, crossed the hall, and entered the room where her stepson was seated, with his back towards the door, and leaning forward with his folded arms on the table. She advanced, holding out her hand,—

"This is an agreeable surprise, Gerald," she said, with an assumption of ease that she did not feel, "I never expected your return so soon as this."

On hearing these words Lord Durant turned round sharply, and she beheld a face that startled her by its alteration; it was not so much the visible sadness as the expression of anger, almost hatred, with which he regarded her.

"You surely do not intend to upbraid me for my son's wickedness!" she exclaimed, retreating a little, with dismay, when she noticed the flashing of the dark eyes that were fixed on her face. "You dare not be so cruel, so unjust, as to add to the trouble it has caused. I would gladly have died before this had happened!"

For a second a slight look of pity softened Lord Durant's stern expression.

"No; I do not blame you for that," he answered, in a low voice; "but does your conscience altogether hold you blameless of injuries and deception towards me? Ah! I see you tremble and grow pale; my words strike home!"

Lady Durant fell on her knees, crouching down in an agony of self-accusation before her stepson.

"Gerald, forgive me!" she implored. "It was for Lionel's sake!"

"Hush! not another word: you are only criminating yourself; I have not stated my accusation yet!" cried Lord Durant, struggling fiercely with the overpowering resentment that he felt; "and you seek to lessen your own base wickedness by such paltry excuses. I know Agatha still lives; I have both seen and spoken with her." He uttered the fact calmly and coldly, all the while facing the wretched woman who was grovelling at his feet. "Sit down there," he added, sternly, pointing to a seat; "it is useless to attempt to soften my heart by tears and entreaties,—you have hardened it too much already; there are other subjects about which I have to speak to you."

Feeling that further attempts to find excuses for her own conduct were both foolish and unnecessary, Lady Durant did as she was desired; she rose tremblingly, and not daring to look up, with all her natural boldness turned into abject cowardice, she stood quietly waiting for him to speak again. Her very silence produced some little pity in Lord Durant's heart; he felt how completely she was in his power: he had expected a fierce denial of his accusation, and now only to meet with an appeal for mercy almost robbed him of self-control.

"Of course I can perceive your motive for this cruel deception," he continued; "it was for the sake of your unworthy son, whom I once called my brother. But why was it that you allowed me to marry when you knew my wife was living?"

"I did not know, indeed I did not!" cried Lady Durant, again instinctively resorting to whatever could serve to hide her guilty conduct. "I had lost sight of her for years. It was her proposal to retire into the convent; I myself heard her express a wish that she might be dead to you—that you might never again behold her: it was partly to secure her happiness that I raised the report of her death!"

"You are only making your conduct appear worse," interrupted the indignant nobleman. "What reason had you to lose sight of Agatha? When I was once more permitted to take up my abode at Pen Vychan, why could you not have told me she still lived? But it is useless to prolong the discussion."

He turned away, and a groan of terrible misery rose to his lips.

"Gerald, cannot you show some forgiveness?" again pleaded Lady Durant. "You, as a father, know what a parent will sacrifice to secure a child's welfare."

A thrill of emotion caused Lord Durant to look up; these words were not without their effect. What had he not sacrificed for his son? he had even (so he believed) given up Mavis's respect and affection for the sake of his own child; and now, when he heard the appeal that moved him so deeply, he felt for a moment as if he could no longer resist his stepmother's entreaty for mercy; but quick as lightning another thought rushed into his brain—one that had occurred to him before.

"I will try and forgive," he answered, speaking slowly and with apparent difficulty, "as far as it is possible to forgive such a fearful wrong; I will do so, if you will answer me one question: it must be truthfully answered, without any attempts at further concealment. What became of my son?"

" Your son—Mervyn—why, you know he died!" said Lady Durant, with vainly assumed astonishment, although the observant eyes that were watching her saw a slowly gathering expression of increased terror.

" You know what I mean," replied Lord Durant, now fairly roused to passion, against which all the while he had been fiercely struggling. "I will have no prevarication. Either you must answer my question, or your request for forgiveness will be totally disregarded. Once more, is my son, Agatha's child, really dead; or if not, what became of him? I have strong reasons to believe he lives. Speak! I will have the truth."

For a minute Lady Durant was unable to reply; she could feel the penetrating glance fixed on her face; it seemed to her as if her thoughts were visible to her indignant accuser. Utterly bewildered and hopeless as she was, she vainly struggled to answer; but the words would not come; bitter sobs choked her utterance.

The nobleman waited patiently until the paroxysm of angry grief was over; it was not in his nature to exult over the distress even of this woman who had brought so much misery.

"Cannot you answer?" he said at length, growing rather impatient at the prolonged silence, that he interpreted as a sign of guilt; she only bent her head lower, and wept more bitterly than ever. "Surely you did not make away with the child?" continued Lord Durant, in a low husky tone, as if he scarcely dared utter aloud the horrible suspicion.

"Oh, no, indeed!" answered his stepmother, raising her head indignantly. "How can you believe it of me? To the best of my belief he still lives."

"Then where is he?" was the stern question.

"I do not know."

"Not know! what do you mean, Lady Durant? Have you added to your wicked conduct by losing sight of one who never wronged or harmed you? Surely you know what became of him! I can bear no more of this deception. Speak! I command you," exclaimed Lord Durant, authoritatively.

It was very humiliating to Lady Durant to feel that each moment was bringing her nearer to full confession. The proud, haughty woman felt subdued and conscience-stricken before him whom she had always despised and hated with all the strength of jealousy. All her courage had disappeared; as he advanced towards her she shrank back with a shriek of mingled dismay and terror. She dreaded his naturally violent temper, expecting every minute to hear him break forth into angry denunciations; but no, the expression of terrible sadness that had struck her so forcibly when she had entered the room was still unchanged, nothing seemed to have the power to rouse him; he stood apparently calm, only demanding an answer to his question, out of justice to his son, who, he knew now, had been kept out of his rights for so many years.

"Do you want to excite suspicion—to let every one in this house know of your crimes?" he asked, as Lady Durant's cry echoed through the room. "Why do you not reply quietly, without making your conduct public?"

A ray of hope brightened the terrified face.

"Gerald, will you—do you intend to preserve it secret?" she asked, eagerly.

"It would be no more than simple justice if I published it to the world," replied Lord Durant. "I cannot altogether keep it from being known, suspicion must necessarily be roused; but I will do what I can,—the name of Durant is already too notorious. You must give me some clue by which I can find my son, and then I shall leave your conscience to do the rest—it will be sufficient punishment; remember that it is owing to your base falsehoods that your son Lionel has proved such a disgrace to the name he bears."

Lady Durant had been expecting reproaches, and these words sounded so mild and forgiving, so different from what she had dared to hope, that their very clemency proved more effectual than the sternest anger could have done.

"Oh, Gerald! how could I ever have behaved so cruelly to you?" she sobbed, without attempting to make further excuses for her wrong-doing. "The child was at Pen Vychan; he was brought up by a servant, Jane Morgan," she continued, raising her head, and facing Lord Durant with a look that showed that she was uttering the truth. "She alone can tell you what has become of him."

"Ah, it is as I suspected!" exclaimed the nobleman, hurriedly. "Give me the woman's address; I will go and obtain full particulars from her. You can write a few words, so as to release her from her promise of secrecy."

As he spoke, Lord Durant placed writing-materials before her, and standing patiently by, waited whilst his stepmother had, with a shaking hand, written a few lines to Mrs. Hughes, such as would be sufficient to draw from her the long-guarded secret. She folded up the note, and, without glancing towards her stepson, placed it in his hands, and then, turning quickly away, to hide the emotion produced by this sudden annihilation of all her hopes, she hurried from the room.

Lord Durant did not attempt to detain her; he had gained all the needful information, and had forced her to confess her guilt. He could realize too fully the struggle she had undergone to care to torment her further, and, after all, his feelings were the most bitter against Lionel. In time, perhaps, he might be able to forgive his stepmother; but his brother had wronged him too deeply for any forgiveness.

"There is the one excuse—her blind affection and ambition for that unworthy son of hers," he thought, as he roused himself to prepare for departure. There was much to be done. He had left Rome on purpose to seek out his son; that purpose had at present only been half accomplished.

Mrs. Melcombe's entrance put an end to his gloomy reverie. She had gathered an indistinct idea of what had happened. Lady Durant's cry, followed by her sudden exit from the library, had aroused her curiosity, and she was eager to learn the truth of what had occurred. There was a peculiar smile on her face as she advanced to greet Lord Durant. "She was so sorry for him; no one could sympathize more deeply in his great trouble than she did," she hastened to explain. "But really she had almost expected it. Poor Lady Durant! Her son's wickedness had nearly broken her heart." Thus she went on, talking rapidly, without perceiving how each word was planting a sharp sting in her auditor's heart, how inexpressibly painful her mistaken attempts at consolation were to him.

She was profuse in her offers of hospitality, pressing Lord Durant to make the Deanery his home for the present, instead of going to the Abbey; "it would be so melancholy for him, all by himself."

All this Lord Durant declined, rather

more decisively than was usual with him. Mrs. Melcombe's manner irritated him beyond endurance.

"I have business which calls me away to Pen Vychan at present," he said. "If that is satisfactorily settled, I hope to come back and take up my permanent abode at St. Hilda's."

No more information could Mrs. Melcombe obtain, and, at length, though sorely against her will, she was compelled to let him depart, leaving her curiosity unsatisfied, but unabated.

"Now I will get to the root of this mystery," she said, when she had talked the occurrence over with Isabel. "By some means or other I will endeavour to find out the secret that exists between Lord Durant and his stepmother. The quarrel certainly cannot be about the major: Lord Durant would not be so wicked as to hold the mother responsible for the son's actions. For my part, I do not like him at all; he is far too proud and overbearing, and presumes too much on his high rank. A man who has spent half his life in a lunatic asylum, and married a low-born actress, ought to be careful how he behaves. I must go now and try to console poor Lady Durant: I dare say he has been abusing and insulting her terribly."

CHAPTER III.

NEW HOPES FOR IVOR.

Lull'd in the countless chambers of the brain,
Our thoughts are link'd by many a hidden chain;
Awake but one, and lo! what myriads rise!
                                                    ROGERS.

ONCE more outside the Deanery doors, Lord Durant breathed freely, although there was a terrible aching at his heart, remorse for the hard part that justice compelled him to play. Had it not been for the suspicions that had been roused in his heart when first the idea had entered it that Ivor was his son, nothing would have induced him to endure the painful interview with his stepmother; but now it was over, and she had confessed, he had nothing more to do but seek the proof that would reinstate his son into his rights.

He pursued his way to the railway station, after several delays; there were so many friends whom he happened to meet, all eager to speak, and, though he noticed saddened, pitying looks on their faces, there was not a word said in allusion to the subject that they all perceived was so painful to him. Seated in the train on his way towards Pen Vychan, he had time to think calmly over the strange whirl of events that had passed so rapidly. He could now permit his mind to realize the fact that his son was living. The evidence was so strong in favour of Ivor being that child as not to admit of a doubt. Before leaving Rome he had closely questioned the young man, and had heard from Claude Montieth that he also entertained the same suspicion, and now he felt it was verified.

And then came a sensation approaching regret. The station in which Ivor had been brought up was so very different to that which he would in future occupy. Certainly he had talent, and the association with Claude Montieth had tended to elevate his mind; but still there was a want of education and refinement, that, although not so apparent in the artist, would be painfully visible in the nobleman's heir, especially to the eyes of his father. But Lord Durant quickly endeavoured to dispel these thoughts.

"I ought to rejoice that there is some one more worthy than Lionel Durant to inherit after me," he thought, reproaching himself for the regrets that he considered wrong to entertain. "It is curious that I should have taken a fancy to the lad, that I should have befriended him, never dreaming that he was my son. I suppose it was the strange likeness that first led me to feel interested in him."

The likeness to Lionel! The very idea sent a stab of horror through the nobleman's heart. What if the resemblance was not only in form and feature, but in character? But on maturer consideration the passing thought was dismissed. Everything he had seen or heard of Ivor was to his credit. Claude had spoken in high terms of his pupil, and had even expressed his gratification that such good fortune would probably fall to the lot of one who deserved it so fully.

And then Lord Durant's mind went back to his first meeting with Ivor; but the reminiscence also brought thoughts of Mavis, recalling the one all-absorbing trouble that he struggled so hard but in vain to banish from his heart. As each moment brought him nearer to Pen Vychan, the place that was most closely associated with recollections of her, the thoughts grew more acute, more intensely painful. It was useless now; no hopes for the future, no attempts to recall the past, could serve to banish the ever-present, ever-torturing misery; and when at last, wearied in mind and body with the long day's travelling and excitement he had undergone, he once more arrived in his native village, he felt as if years had passed since he last beheld the familiar spot.

The long, bright summer day was nearly over, the last golden rays of the setting sun were fast disappearing, as he walked along the street, feeling wretched and dispirited, undecided even where to go. The Castle had been let to strangers. From where he stood he could see the smoke curling up from the chimneys amongst the trees, and a chill sense of complete loneliness struck him. It seemed just then as if he were utterly, entirely alone in the world. But it was getting late, and the object of his journey was still unaccomplished; so, mustering up all his energies, he set out to walk towards David Hughes's farm, along the well-remembered winding road, every step of which was familiar to him. He preferred to go on foot, for the distance was not great, and the cool sea breeze was pleasant after the heat of the day. About half an hour's brisk walking brought him within sight of the low white buildings, and before he reached them Lord Durant espied the farmer himself, standing smoking in the doorway after his day's work was over.

"Good evening, Hughes," he began. "Is your wife at home? I wish to speak to her."

The farmer turned round, and taking his pipe from his mouth, stared at the nobleman with unconcealed astonishment.

"Why, my lord, I thought you were in foreign parts!" he exclaimed. "Who would have thought of seeing you here! But will you do me the honour to walk in? My wife is in the dairy, and I'll call her."

He held the door open for his visitor to pass into the large kitchen, and then, opening another door, he called out, "Jane, you are wanted."

"Who is it? Tell them to wait," called out another voice.

Instantly the portly figure of David Hughes disappeared through the doorway, and some loud whispering ensued, which scarcely reached Lord Durant's ears, and presently Mrs. Hughes herself came in, wiping her hands on her apron and curtseying, profuse in her apologies to his lordship for keeping him waiting. "But, you see, I was just making up the butter ready for tomorrow's market; we have to send it off so early to get to Rhos Celyn in time, so I hope you'll excuse me, my lord?"

"Yes, certainly, Mrs. Hughes," replied Lord Durant. "But my business with you can soon be transacted. I believe you were once in the service of my wife, Lady Durant, at Pen Vychan Castle?"

"Yes, my lord, so I was, eighteen years ago or more. Time passes, and we none of us get younger, as your lordship, I dare say, knows. It was a very good place, and her ladyship was a kind mistress. It isn't many of the quality that will take back an old servant when she's a lone widow, as I was, with scarce a friend in the world."

"Yes, yes, my good woman, I understand all this," interrupted the nobleman, rather impatiently. "I think before we proceed to business you had better read this," and he handed his stepmother's letter to her.

She slowly read the contents, and Lord Durant, watching her face, noticed it turn very pale.

"Oh, my lord, I didn't mean to do wrong," she exclaimed, in a voice of real terror. Oh, don't send me to gaol! I'll never do it again! But she told me it would never be found out; that it wasn't a crime; and I was poor, and the money tempted me."

"You acknowledge that you were bribed to take away the child from its mother, and deceive her by telling her it was dead," said Lord Durant; "and all this time you have kept the fact from me that my son was living? Why do you ask for pity? why do you seek to make excuses for your wickedness?"

"No, my lord, indeed it wasn't as bad as that. My own baby was dead, and I was fretting sorely about it, although I didn't know what would become of me; for if it hadn't have been for her ladyship's kindness I must have been in the workhouse. And then Lady Durant—the old lady I mean—came and spoke so kindly, and promised me all sorts of things if I'd only do what she wanted. She paid me the money, and brought the little new-born baby, and I took to it; it was a comfort to me, for I knew I'd got plenty of money then; and so, you see, I couldn't help keeping the secret."

"And so you brought up the child as your own?" continued Lord Durant, as soon as the woman had finished her almost incoherent narrative, which was related with frequent bursts of tears and appeals for mercy.

"Yes, my lord, at least for a time; and everybody thought he was mine, even my husband's father; but then when Hughes came courting me he said that he did not want other people's children; and, as old Mr. Morgan offered to take Ivor, I let him go, for you see, my lord, I never could come to think of him as one of my own."

All this time David Hughes had been standing by listening with an incredulous stare of bewilderment to the conversation between his wife and Lord Durant; to his mind it seemed an inexplicable mystery, and it was some time before he began to arrive at the truth that the nobleman's questions were fast drawing from the terrified woman.

"What do you mean?" he cried, at last, in loud, angry tones. "Is it true that your Ivor is no child of yours, but his lordship's? Why, Jane, I wouldn't have believed that you would have gone on all these years keeping the lad out of his rights."

His indignation was roused, but Lord Durant hastened to interpose; he was feeling an unaccountable weariness and disgust at the force of circumstances that caused him to turn accuser. Staying only to ask a few more necessary questions, he took his departure with a feeling of thankfulness that he had gained all the information he required; and it was with a lighter heart that he retraced his steps to the village. It was proved now beyond doubt that Ivor was his son, and the mere knowledge that there was an heir to his property and name was in itself a source of comfort to him. And as he walked along he found himself even making plans for the future, and speculating on Ivor's surprise when he should hear of his good fortune.

"I wish I knew more of the lad," he said to himself; "if his looks do not belie him he has the making of a fine character. I certainly like what I have seen of him, especially his spirited defence of Agatha's conduct — his mother. How strange it seems that they should meet as they did in a foreign land! it is all so wonderful. I can scarcely even realize it yet."

His musings were suddenly interrupted by the appearance of a familiar figure advancing towards him. He immediately recognized Mr. Williams.

"Why, Lord Durant, I never expected to see you here at this hour!" exclaimed the clergyman, as they shook hands. "I did not even know that you were in England."

"I came home this morning," replied the nobleman: "and since then I have heard news that has induced me to come to Pen Vychan. But surely you have heard—about my dreadful trouble, I mean," he added, with an effort; for even to allude to Mavis was more than he could bear.

"Yes, yes, we have heard. It was of course a heavy trial to us, and must be a still more painful subject to you," replied Mr. Williams, hurriedly. "I am sure you have our fullest sympathy. I could scarcely have believed that my sister's child could be so wicked."

"Do not blame her! I cannot bear it

yet!" cried Lord Durant, and a spasm of pain crossed his features. "It is all too fresh and vivid in my mind; perhaps time will soften the blow, but at present it is too much."

Mr. Williams was silent, out of pity for his evident distress, and the nobleman continued, in an altered voice of forced composure,—

"My visit to Pen Vychan is a purely business one; and you, if you will, can give me some information."

"Certainly, Lord Durant, anything that lies in my power you may be sure I will do. But will you come home with me? You look as if you stand in need of rest and refreshment."

The nobleman hesitated for a second, and then accepted the proffered hospitality. The fatigue of the day was beginning to tell on him, and in his present mood he was longing for some one to whom he could confide his discovery concerning his long-lost son. At first there was a momentary sensation of reluctance to put himself under even so slight an obligation to one of Mavis's relatives, but he quickly dismissed the idea with scorn, as one unworthy to be entertained.

He followed the clergyman into the homely little dwelling. Mr. Williams listened with some surprise to what he had to say, making no comments, for he plainly perceived how anxious Lord Durant was to shield his stepmother. "I have been to Mrs. Hughes, and she has confirmed Lady Durant's words," added the nobleman, as soon as he had finished the account.

"Mrs. Hughes is not a parishioner of mine, but I am acquainted with her; and her heartless conduct to her supposed son has often struck me as very strange, but now of course it is accounted for," replied Mr. Williams, when he had recovered a little from the bewilderment that the sudden disclosure had caused.

In an instant his thoughts flew to his daughter Jessie, and her love for Ivor; for although she rarely mentioned his name, and, obedient to her promise, never attempted to write to him, her father could easily perceive that her affection for her young lover was as strong as ever,—it was not a mere girlish romance; and now he began to blame himself for having ridiculed and opposed them.

"If I could only have foreseen what was to happen!" he said to himself; but his ambitious thoughts were dispelled by the nobleman's next words, uttered in a tone of reproach.

"Mr. Williams, cannot you find some words of congratulation to me on finding my son? You have so long known and taken an interest in him that you ought to feel glad; or are you afraid that altered fortunes may prove hurtful to him?"

"Not in the least; I am certain of it," exclaimed the clergyman, excitedly. "If ever there was a young man worthy to adorn a higher station it is Ivor Morgan. I have known him all his life, and have always felt the greatest esteem for him; he has had many temptations to draw him from the path of honesty, but has steadily resisted them all."

At this moment Mrs. Williams entered the room. She had heard of Lord Durant's arrival, and brought little Maud Austin to see him.

Occupied as his mind was with other topics, the nobleman had partially forgotten the existence of the child; at least, on coming to Mr. Williams's house he had not recollected that he should meet her there. The sight of her, with the strong likeness to Mavis, caused a throb of anguish, which, however, he quickly stifled, as the child uttered a cry of joy on perceiving him.

"Have you come to take me home? Oh, I am so glad!" she exclaimed, as he took her tiny hand, and, drawing her towards him, kissed her tenderly, for his kind heart was touched with pity for the friendless little orphan.

"Should you like to go back with me?" he asked, with a sad smile, for the child had clasped her arms round his neck and was clinging to him. There was something soothing to his aching heart even in the love of this child.

"Yes; don't go without me; take me with you," she resumed, with pleading accents.

"For shame, Maud! I think you are an ungrateful little girl to want to leave us," said Mrs. Williams, approaching to take the child from Lord Durant, but she turned round and raised her little hand in a fury of anger.

"Go away! you shan't touch me!" she exclaimed, passionately. "You are a naughty woman; you said that Mavis was wicked, and you wished she was dead. It's very cruel, because she loved me. You won't call my sister wicked, will you?" she asked, looking with a gentler expression into Lord Durant's face.

"No, no, my darling!" replied the nobleman, in a voice scarcely audible from emotion, as he held the child closer to him, feeling that she formed a link between him and the shattered love that he could not banish from his heart. "Yes, you shall go home with me to St. Hilda's, and be my own little girl."

"And can Jessie come too?" asked Maud, quickly.

"Yes, if she likes; Jessie shall come and

stay with you," was the reply; and then, turning to Mrs. Williams, he added, "Please do not be offended if I take this little one from under your care. I am a foolish old man, no doubt, but I cannot bear the thought of the dreary, empty home."

"Certainly we shall not be offended. Of course Maud's interests can be better taken care of with you than with us," the clergyman said, rather stiffly; "but you will have your son."

"Oh, yes—Ivor; but it is different," answered Lord Durant, shaking his head sadly. "I am afraid that between me and my son there can be but little in common, although for his sake I must strive not to show that I perceive it."

And then, refusing Mr. Williams's pressing invitation to remain for the night, Lord Durant started (in the carriage that had brought him) back again to Rhos Celyn, after having promised to make arrangements for the reception of Maud at the Abbey. He inquired after Jessie, but learned that she had gone to visit some friends, so that he was obliged to depart without seeing her.

When he was gone, Mr. Williams told his wife the discovery of Ivor's parentage. It was a fact that concerned them deeply on Jessie's account. Mrs. Williams was inclined to blame her husband for having refused to sanction the engagement. "But," she added, "who could have foreseen, that he would turn out to be the son of a nobleman? I can scarcely believe it myself. I hope Lord Durant will remember his promise to the child and invite Jessie to St. Hilda's; it is only due to her, after the trouble she has had with Maud all these months. She would meet Ivor there, and then who knows what might happen?"

CHAPTER IV.

STRICKEN WITH GRIEF.

Swiftly our pleasures glide away,
Our hearts recall the distant day
　　With many sighs;
The moments that are speeding fast
We heed not, but the past—the past—
　　More highly prize.
LONGFELLOW.

THE brief period of anxious excitement that had ended with Lord Durant's interview with Mrs. Hughes, and the discovery that his son was living, had for a time served to divert his mind from the contemplation of his terrible grief; but this soon passed away, and the reaction came with twofold violence, overwhelming him with crushing sorrow. He returned to St. Hilda's, mechanically seeking the place that he had come to regard as home, but it was a home robbed of all its sunshine and delight. Without Mavis, what was even his life worth? There was nothing but blank, horrible despair to look forward to in the future. He longed for death to end the torture of existence.

There was only one bright spot in the dreary, cheerless picture. The title and estates that he was proud to think he had never dishonoured would pass into other hands than those of the brother who was so unworthy to bear them. His last effort, before he finally succumbed beneath the weight of misery, was to write to Ivor, to recall him to the home of his ancestors, and then, perhaps happily for himself, a severe illness brought a respite to the overtaxed brain by producing a long period of mental oblivion.

And Ivor, after having imparted the strange and wonderful news to his mother, who was rejoiced to welcome him, whom she already loved, as her son, took leave of his friends in Rome and hastened to obey his father's request.

All through the journey his mind was filled with the new and delightful thoughts produced by the unexpected good fortune that had befallen him. He could scarcely realize that he, a poor, obscure artist, could so suddenly have risen to rank and wealth so far exceeding his most sanguine day-dreams of future greatness: he—the heir to the Durant estates, the son of his former benefactor!—it seemed incredible! And yet the consciousness of the entire change gave a new dignity and a sense of power, that was pleasant to one whose ambition had always been to raise himself above the station in which he had been brought up.

As the train sped on, each moment bringing him nearer to St. Hilda's, he grew more excited, with an eager longing to behold the home in which his life would be spent. At length the dense cloud that always hung like a canopy over the city came in sight, and presently Ivor could distinguish the massive, weather-stained towers of the Cathedral standing out against the clear evening sky.

His thoughts reverted to the time when he had first beheld them; when, poor, friendless, and lonely, struggling against the despair produced by the hopelessness of his love for Jessie, he had passed through the same country over which he was now travelling, but with such different feelings! It almost bewildered him to recall them, and to contrast the happiness of the present with the gloomy past.

The sight of the old city, with its quaint mixture of venerable artistic glory, and the huge factories built so close to these decaying evidences of the former wealth and importance of its inhabitants, brought an expression of thought and sadness to his handsome features, and softened the look of enthusiasm that had illumined his face on the first sight of the walls, under the shadow of which his ancestors had dwelt for centuries.

Sybil had told him of the work of improvement that Lord Durant had striven to carry out; and all she had said about it, her praises of the self-sacrifice that the nobleman had shown, now returned to his mind, and brought with it a steadfast resolve that his energies, from that time, ought also to be devoted to the same work. The new life that he was about to take up must not be merely one of self-gratification, but of real, earnest assistance to the parent to whom he owed so much.

And then came the slackening of the speed, and in a moment after the ringing of a bell announced the arrival at the station. Almost before the train stopped Ivor sprang out on to the platform and looked around, expecting some one to meet him; but there were no familiar faces, no carriage waiting for him. It caused a slight depression, and almost a sensation of shyness, at having to take his way alone and unwelcomed to his father's house.

"Can he have received the letter that I wrote to announce the time of my coming?" he asked himself, as he threaded his way through the narrow, familiar streets; but Ivor was not much given to conjecture; he walked on, swiftly passed under the old arched gateway, and it was with a thrill of exultation, such as he had never before experienced, that he pursued his way beneath the shade of the venerable trees, which now assumed a peculiar charm to him. Even he himself was surprised at the keen, eager interest with which he gazed around. The weird, almost melancholy-looking landscape was invested with a strange significance; the grand forms of the giant oaks roused his artistic nature to admiration, whilst in his ears sounded the roar of furnaces and the din of forges, all tending to rouse his brain to a pitch of hitherto unknown excitement. They spoke to him of decaying beauties of the past, and pointed towards work, and the stern, unlovely reality of a toiling existence, in which it would be his highest duty and privilege to make the interest of the future.

He stood before the heavy oak door, pausing a moment to turn again and gaze back before he could summon courage to make his presence known. The servant who opened the door did not know him; he

had evidently not been informed of his
young master's coming. His lordship was
ill," he said; "but would the young gentleman walk in?" and Ivor, half-mechanically,
obeyed the invitation and followed the footman into the library. There, standing alone,
trembling with excitement, and perhaps a
little disappointment at the cheerless welcome, his eye fell on his own letter—the one
he had written from Rome—lying unopened
on the table. So no one had known of his
coming; he was not expected, he thought,
as he walked to the window, with a heavy
weight at his heart, and a sinking, depress-
ing sense of mortification. He did not hear
the door open, or the approach of a light
step; he was occupied in gazing out, as if
all his mind were absorbed in contemplation
of the distant view; and then a low, gentle
voice, the sound of which caused his heart to
beat wildly, addressed him by name. He
turned round suddenly, his face all at once
transformed with hope and joy, and in
another moment he had taken both of
Jessie's hands in his, and was looking down

into her face with all the affection of his ardent love.

"Oh, Jessie! Jessie! and this is our long hoped-for meeting!" he cried. There were tears standing in her eyes as she raised them to his, with a look that emboldened him to steal his arm round her waist, and press loving kisses on her lips. "My love!—my dearest! they will not wish to separate us now," he continued. "You have heard who I really am; and, oh, the joy that you should be the first to welcome me to my home!"

"Yes, Ivor, Lord Durant told me this morning; I did not know before, for he has been very, very ill; you cannot imagine how he has suffered. Oh, it was terrible to witness such misery, and to know that nothing could be done to soften the blow; but come, I will go and tell him of your arrival; he did not expect you so soon."

As Jessie spoke she moved towards the door, but before reaching it she turned back to Ivor. With the tears still glistening in her eyes, but a bright, happy smile on her lips, she exclaimed impulsively,—

"I am so glad it has happened, Ivor, it seems too good to be really true!"

It was so like the old child-like manner of the peaceful Pen Vychan days that Ivor could scarcely forbear a smile. She was very little changed, the same truthful honest blue eyes, and round, cheerful face, now beaming with unconcealed happiness at the reunion with her young lover and companion of bygone times; she looked up, and scanned his features with a feeling of awe; she noticed the visible alteration, the refinement that the change of associations had produced in his appearance; there was something noble in Ivor's face and figure that marked him out from amongst his fellow creatures; there was an unmistakable stamp of genius in the clear broad forehead and large dark eyes, that had been strengthened and increased since the brilliant artistic nature had been fostered and called forth.

"Oh, Ivor, what a *grand* gentleman you have become!" she cried, enthusiastically, clasping her hands together in the excess of her outspoken admiration. "I should scarcely have known you again."

He smiled fondly, and kissed her again, not without a secret feeling of gratification at her last words, and then, speaking in an altered tone, he resumed,—

"And what is this I hear about the illness of my father?—although it seems strange to call him by that name yet. Do you know, I sometimes feel a presentiment as if this bright dream is all a delusion, that I shall wake up and find myself plain Ivor Morgan, a poor fisherman, vainly struggling against the hopeless affection for the dearest, brightest little creature in existence. Come, tell me about it; and why are you at the abbey? I am anxious to know everything."

As he said this Ivor took a seat, and drew Jessie towards him, whilst he waited for her reply.

"I think it is trouble and sorrow that has brought on this illness. It is all through Mavis's cruelty," she said, sinking her voice to a whisper, as if she could not bear to utter her cousin's name aloud. "He never speaks of her, but it is easy to see that he cannot forget, even for one moment. I do not think we can understand how he feels her loss; and I fancy his love for her has not altogether gone—I am sure that poor little Maud's likeness to her sister is the sole reason that makes him more contented when the child is with him: he has seemed more peaceful ever since we came to the Abbey. I am here as Maud's governess," she added; "it was very kind of Lord Durant, wasn't it? because I am so young for such a position: but Maud was anxious for me to remain with her. Poor little child! I would do anything to give her pleasure."

The unexpected meeting with Jessie had reassured Ivor, and served, in some measure, to prepare him for the meeting with his father, which, in spite of his excitement, he had been anticipating with a sensation approaching to dread. Many times during the journey he had wondered with what sort of welcome he should meet. It had never even occurred to his mind to picture to himself the dim, gloomy chamber in which the interview really took place; the pale, still form, the well-remembered and already beloved features, nearly as white as the pillow on which they rested.

Lord Durant moved his position, and raised his weary eyes to Ivor's face when the young man entered, pale and awe-stricken, scarcely daring even to intrude into the presence of such visible sorrow and suffering. He tried to speak, but the words failed him; it was all he could do to subdue the wild beating of his heart and the emotion that caused him to tremble so violently. But his father's mournful, dark eyes were fixed on his face, and from them shone, for one second, a slight expression of hope.

"It is good of you to come," was all he said, in a low voice, whose altered tones caused a thrill of pity in Ivor's heart; but the kind, grateful pressure of his hand spoke more eloquently than words could do; and then he turned his head away, and again the stony look of despair crept over the still pale face.

The physician had remained in the room;

he now advanced towards Ivor, who stood silent and motionless by the bedside, gazing down sorrowfully at the wasted, altered features, and beckoned him away.

"Oh, what is it? Is he dying?" were the words that broke from Ivor's lips as soon as the door was closed behind them, the grave look on his companion's face alarming him even more than the sight he had just beheld.

The physician shook his head.

"The illness is more of the mind than the body, I fear," he said, with an emphasis on the last word that Ivor was quick to detect. "It is your coming that we have hoped for as the best means of alleviating his suffering. No doubt his greeting appears cold to you; but I fancy that Lord Durant feels more acutely than we can imagine."

It was with a saddened feeling that Ivor returned to the library. He had come to St. Hilda's full of bright hopes for the future. Everything that he could desire had seemed as if it would speedily be realized in the dazzling splendour of the good fortune that had overtaken him; and now had come a complete downfall of his hopes: his happiness had received a sudden check.

He knew enough of his father's former life to feel certain that the fiery trials had reduced him to a state of despair from which he might never be roused, and that at any moment the power of self-control might vanish, and the good, true, unselfish heart was breaking beneath the weight with which it had been burdened. The loving, trustful soul had been betrayed and tortured by cruel caprice and heartless wickedness. And from that time, at the outset of a perfectly new life, Ivor made a firm resolve to remain steadfast to the duties that so urgently presented themselves before him.

In quitting Rome he knew that he had given up the profession that he loved and rejoiced in, with all the ardour of genius; it was probably gone from him for ever now he had taken up new responsibilities the foremost of which was to strive to render his father's melancholy, embittered existence as happy as possible.

By degrees the first shyness and constraint

produced by Ivor's altered fortunes began to wear off, especially when signs of amendment showed themselves in Lord Durant's state, and gradually the stricken mind awoke to what was going on round him, and showed some little interest in the affairs of others, but it was long before danger was pronounced to be over. Many weeks of terrible anxiety and heart-rending suspense had to be endured, before the slightest hope of Lord Durant's recovery had entered the hearts of those who, day by day, witnessed the sufferings that were too intense for realization. And thus sympathy and grief did the work that would have been impossible in the midst of prosperity. It served to strengthen the mutual confidence that had arisen in the first days of doubt and dreadful fear following the discovery of Mavis's flight, and, before long, Ivor's true goodness of heart and thoughtful care had gained the affection of the parent from whom he had so long been separated.

Lord Durant was not ungrateful: it did not take him long to discover that, in giving up his artist's life, Ivor's heart still remained true to his old friends, and little by little he managed to draw from him a true account of the state of poverty to which the Montieths had been reduced by Claude's failing health; and before the long summer days had given place to the mellow tints of the approaching harvest season, the young man found an interest in superintending the furnishing of the little dwelling that he had been allowed to select for his friend's occupation; for Claude was coming home: he had gladly responded to Lord Durant's wish that he should return to St. Hilda's, the nobleman having promised to secure for his son's friend the patronage of the most influential people in the neighbourhood. Even the invalid was roused to animation when he watched the joyous excitement that the power of conferring happiness on others produced in his son. It struck a chord of sympathy in his heart, and lent a fresh stimulus invoked by the discovery of similitude in their characters. It was the beginning of a renewal of his former work and interests, and soon the poorer inhabitants of St. Hilda's were able to welcome their former benefactor back to the scene of his labours; but no assurance of the benefits he was able to confer could draw a smile from that stern mouth, or dispel for one instant the haggard, careworn look that was now habitual to him. The name of Lord Durant was uttered everywhere with praises, but it was in a low, hushed tone, as if it were sacrilege to allude to the grief about which he never spoke, and so he went through his self-imposed duties, solitary and lonely, for Ivor, who fain would help him, was away at the University, where his father had sent him to complete his education in order to fit him for the duties and responsibilities that some day would devolve on him.

CHAPTER V.

SEEN FROM THE STREET.

Didst thou but know how pale I sat at home,
My eyes still turned the way thou wert to come;
And all the long, long nights of hope and fear,
Thy voice and step still sounding in my ear.
MOORE.

A YEAR and a half had passed away, and the London season was at its height; a sudden downfall of rain had driven the crowd of pleasure-seekers into shelter, and caused those who were out on business to hurry over their respective errands: the wet conveyances drove by, and the passengers with dripping umbrellas jostled each other on the pavement, all presenting a scene of discomfort to the eyes of a lovely watcher, in a room on the ground-floor of well-furnished apartments not far from Sloane Square.

For hours she had sat by that window in a weary, despairing attitude of disappointed expectation. The evening came on, and still she remained at her post; the street-lamps were lit. the one on the opposite side shone into the room, lighting up the solitary figure, only partially concealed from the gaze of the passers-by by the folds of the lace curtains.

She did not move from her position; she paid no attention to the fact of the growing darkness, only shuddered slightly when the chimes from a neighbouring church proclaimed the passing hours. It was not until a servant entered to light the gas that she rose from her seat, and, dashing away the tears, moved to the other side of the room to hide the evidence of her grief from the woman's curious gaze, and throwing herself back on a couch she took up a book, and soon became so absorbed in its contents that for a time her anxiety was forgotten.

Eighteen months, with all their joys and

sorrows had passed over Mavis's fair head, there was still the same angelic beauty of form and feature, perhaps a shade more sad and pensive; but as her eyes, half veiled by their long lashes, with the tears still glistening on them, rested on the open page before her, and with slightly parted lips, and occasional flushes of excited expectation on her cheeks, she presented a picture of perfect loveliness. Page after page of the book did she turn over, until a sound came that caused her heart to beat wildly; she sprang to her feet, trembling in every limb with excitement, and stood motionless for a second as the door opened and admitted the tall, soldierly figure of Major Durant.

"Lionel! Lionel!" she exclaimed, "why, oh, why did you stay away from me for so long?"

He held her in his arms, and bent down and kissed her rosy lips.

"I am glad to be again with you, my little Mavis," he said, with a tender look of affection that drove away all her cares. "I was detained at my club, and am later than usual. Make haste and give me a cup of tea. I have promised to be at Lady Newton's ball this evening."

The radiant countenance fell, the tears again dimmed the eyes that a moment before had been gazing up with an almost worshipping love into the face, one smile from which was more than all the world to her, happy in the affection that had caused her to renounce her friends, self-esteem, and good name, to throw herself on the mercy of this man, who had trifled with her unquestioning, absorbing love. But it all vanished at the sound of his words,—

"Going out again to-night, Lionel? Cannot you spare one evening to stay with me? it used not to be so," she said, in a strangely altered voice. "Before we came to London we were always together, and I was so happy! I wish we had remained on the Continent."

"My darling, you do not understand," Major Durant replied, drawing her nearer to him, for she had moved away towards the tea-table. "I cannot afford to lose my place in society; I am gradually working my way towards a complete reconciliation with my mother. You may rely upon it that a quiet evening with you would be infinitely more to my taste than Lady Newton's crowded hot rooms."

"Oh, Lionel, why cannot you give me the right of going with you? why is it that I am shut out from sharing your pleasures? We are both free; when will you fulfil your often-repeated promise of making me your wife?" she asked, wearily. "It is very hard that I should have to drag on a solitary existence in these dismal rooms, whilst you can mix in all the world's gaiety."

"Why, my poor little woman, what is the cause of these tears?" asked the major, in a low, caressing voice, as if he were soothing a child's troubles. "Cannot you have a little patience? Everything will come right in the end; we have only to wait and hope. Surely your love for me is strong enough to stand a short delay! I thought you cared for me sufficiently to disdain the paltry opinions of society."

"And so I do,—you ought to know that; but oh, you cannot think how I long for the time to come when I need no longer feel this shame, this necessity for concealment. Lionel, my husband, for I ought to call you by that name, I have sacrificed all for love of you."

It was with gentle, loving words, such as he knew so well how to use, that Major Durant attempted to calm the sudden outburst of grief, and Mavis again listened to the empty, meaningless promises that she had so often heard before, but still they found their way to her trustful nature, and she believed in them, falling as they did from his lips. It mattered not that she had been deceived by his fair-sounding phrases; they still served their purpose, and produced forgetfulness of the wrongs of the past in the delirious happiness of the present love, to which the whole thoughts of her existence were abandoned. And when he was gone it seemed as if some sunlight had been taken from her soul; she could scarcely realize that so few moments before she had felt happy in the transitory delight that had so soon passed away.

Her strong affection had survived and triumphed over many severe shocks during the time that they had spent together in the pleasant German cities, and still remained unchanged; but when Lionel had brought her to London her spirits had begun to droop, as she awoke to the fact that she was now no longer the first in his thoughts; he had returned into the midst of his old associations, from which, for a time, he had voluntarily withdrawn.

Now all the notoriety which had attached itself to his name had died away; other topics occupied the public mind, and his friends were eager to welcome the agreeable, fascinating Major Durant once more amongst them. Slowly, almost imperceptibly, the sense of Lionel's growing neglect stole into Mavis's mind; the claims of society were alienating him from her, and many were the bitter tears she shed when alone, soon however to be dispelled by his return.

Meanwhile Lionel Durant was threading

his way amongst the select company that were assembled in Lady Newton's elegant reception-rooms. He never gave a thought during that brilliant evening to the affectionate little creature who was breaking her heart for love of him. In the midst of the lively ball-room conversation, in the whirling dance to the inspiriting strains of a first-rate band, who would think of Mavis, she whose very name could be no more mentioned?

Major Durant was rich now; a wealthy relative of his mother's, one whom the dowager Lady Durant had been content to ignore as having earned his fortune by trade, had lately died and left his nephew a large fortune, and now many match-making mothers with marriageable daughters found it convenient to forget the stain on his character, and once more extend a cordial welcome to the rich, handsome young officer.

"Why, Major Durant, who would have thought of seeing you here to-night?"

Lionel was just leading one of Lady Newton's daughters to her seat, after a waltz, when these words fell on his ear; he turned round and perceived Mrs. Melcombe standing at his elbow.

"I have been watching you for some time, expecting you to come up and speak to us. Have you forgotten your old friends?" she continued, extending her hand.

Her cordiality completely took the major aback for a second; he stammered forth an apology, but instantly recovering his self-possession, he entered into conversation with as much apparent show of friendly feeling as if they had parted but a week before, and Lionel learned that Mrs. Melcombe had only left St. Hilda's on the previous day in order to visit his mother.

"Isabel, my dear, come here and be re-introduced to an old friend," she called out to a tall, handsome girl who was passing, and Isabel Ingram, looking more stately and beautiful than ever, turned from the partner on whose arm she was leaning and advanced towards him. Her habitual haughtiness relaxed, and one of her rare smiles lit up her fine features, as Lionel led her off for the next dance, and soon they were whirling round together, the centre of observation, acknowledged by all as the handsomest couple in the room.

It was not often that Isabel Ingram was so gracious as she was that evening; there were many who envied Major Durant the favour that she showed him, for her beauty always received its share of homage, and she rarely unbent from her stately *hauteur* to any of her numerous admirers, as she was evidently doing then.

"Miss Ingram grows handsomer every day," he whispered to his mother, as he took leave of her; for Lady Durant's maternal affection had not withstood her son's appeal to be received back into her favour.

The dowager smiled as he uttered these words; they presented a deep significance to her mind. It had always been a wish of hers that her son should take a fancy to Isabel; of Mavis no thought ever entered her head; she did not even know that she was in London. Lionel had led her to believe that his love for her was a thing of the past.

And as Major Durant drove along through the London streets that night he was deep in thought. New complications and perplexities had arisen, and he was revolving in his mind plans, which, if Mavis could have guessed them, would have driven her to distraction with grief and horror.

There was one dark spot in his life which he fain would have buried in oblivion. Each day, as he thought of Mavis's tender love, which was worthier of a nobler object, his heart smote him with a vague sensation of self-reproach. He strove against this feeling; there were duties he owed to society, he tried to argue with himself, as he responded to his mother's repeated invitations, and passed morning after morning in Isabel's company. Surely it was no treason to Mavis, he repeatedly told himself; he could admire Isabel; it would not lessen his affection for the little creature whose presence in London he kept such a profound secret from all his friends.

And so time went on; the visits to Mavis were fewer and more hurried.

She perceived his preoccupation, and her heart grew heavier with sadness when she awoke to the fact of his increasing indifference.

It was through overhearing a conversation between the landlady and a friend that Mavis first learned that Major Durant's name was coupled with Miss Ingram's, and herself spoken of with pity that rendered the sting worse to bear. It was the heaviest trial that had yet befallen her—worse than taunts, anger, or reproaches would have been, for it roused the bitter passion of jealousy, and the remnant of hope to which she still vainly clung was rudely torn away.

Trembling with a vague sensation of hopeless unreality, she stood rooted to the spot outside the door, through which the sounds of the conversation reached her.

"Poor thing, one can't help being sorry for her," she heard the landlady's voice declare, "although, if I'd have known what she was, she'd never have darkened my doors; however, it's he that led her astray, no doubt of that; and so young and pretty as she is!—it's a cruel shame! I wonder if she knows that it's said he is engaged to that Miss Ingram. I've noticed her getting paler and sadder looking, as if her heart's breaking with his neglect, and she so soon to be a mother. I'm sure I cannot help pitying her, although one ought not to do so."

This was all Mavis heard, but it was more than enough. She stole noiselessly back into her sitting-room, feeling as if her heart was turned to stone. In those few minutes she had passed through a whole lifetime of anguish, rendered more poignant by the unreasoning jealousy that was tearing at her heart. Her idol had fallen from its high standard. Her life's happiness was crushed and broken, and she was alone, worse than alone, for she had not that love which, until now, she had blindly believed was still hers.

There was to be a large ball that evening, to which many of the *élite* in London had been invited. Lionel, she knew, would be there, for the last week he had been staying at his mother's house, and during that time

Mavis had only received one short visit from him.

"And *she* will be there, too! All his thoughts will be for her, and I shall be forgotten!" she cried aloud, starting to her feet with a gesture of despair. "Oh, Lionel, why was it that I could be induced to sacrifice my whole life to meet with this return!"

The fiery, impulsive nature that had never known control was fully roused; the intensity of her love increased the fierceness of the resentment against him who had betrayed and deceived her.

And then a morbid restlessness seized her; she longed to behold him once more, to prove the truth of the suspicions she had overheard. She knew where to find the house to which he had gone; and perhaps, standing in the darkness of the street, she might get one glance of the face that she so inexpressibly desired, and yet dreaded to see.

A few moments after, wrapped in a long, dark cloak, with a thick veil almost completely obscuring her features, she was threading her way along the gas-lit streets. She felt strangely weary, and yet an invisible power urged her on until she reached the spot where a stream of carriages was waiting before the door of a mansion.

There was the usual crowd to watch the company alight, and, mingling with it, Mavis took up her position close to the portico, where through the open windows she could discern the figures passing and re-passing in the ball-room.

At length a well-known carriage drove up, and for a second she caught sight of Lionel's face. Involuntarily she shrank back, for it seemed as if his eyes were fixed on her, as if he could single her out from amongst that dense throng, and for a moment a mist obscured her sight. She turned sick with horror as she perceived the smile and the look of tender attention with which he turned towards Isabel to assist her from the vehicle. Not an expression or gesture was lost. Mavis noticed the trembling of the small, elegantly gloved hand that was laid in his, the haughty eyes beaming with devotion as the low-toned voice addressed her. They passed so close to her, that the floating clouds of tulle touched her dress as Isabel swept by. An almost incontrollable impulse seized her to spring forward and declare who she was; and, throwing herself at Isabel's feet, reveal the villainy of the man with whom she was talking so confidingly. But just at that moment Major Durant raised his head, seeming to take in the whole surroundings at a glance, and the impulse vanished. Before that look Mavis was powerless to act or think. She could not forget so easily; even jealousy was not strong enough to conquer her love.

When she looked up again they were gone from her sight, and had passed into the brilliantly lighted ball-room, of which she could just catch a glimpse.

The hours rolled slowly by, the outside crowd gradually grew thinner, the carriages had almost ceased to roll, but still Mavis kept her position in front of the house, pacing slowly up and down the pavement, listening with a dull, aching despair to the lively strains of music. She could see Lionel's tall figure amongst the dancers, and occasionally Isabel's graceful form passed the window, and still the lonely watcher remained at her post. The evening grew still and quiet, and several of the guests came out on to the balcony, to enjoy the cool atmosphere; she could even hear the low tones of their conversation.

At length they all returned to the dance, except one couple, and it was on those that her eyes were riveted. The moon shone straight down on Isabel's upturned face, and as the major bent over her his own was shrouded in darkness. It seemed to Mavis as if her senses were preternaturally sharpened, for she could even see the expression that was in her rival's eyes, and Lionel's low-spoken words fell distinctly on her ears.

She had heard the same words before, but oh, what a different significance they had when they were intended for another! She was unable to move; an irresistible fascination chained her to the spot, where her eyes and ears received confirmation of her most terrible fears. The sight of Isabel's pure statuesque beauty almost drove her to frenzy! it was such a contrast to her own fair loveliness that he had declared to be unsurpassable, but it was forgotten now in the fascination of those brilliant dark eyes that smiled and sparkled as they were raised to his.

Presently a sound in the room from which they had come caused Isabel to turn her head.

"Hark! they are coming up from the supper-room," she said. "Lionel, had not we better go inside?"

With languid grace she rose from her seat, and they re-entered the house through the open French window. Lionel's arm was round her waist. Mavis could see his face bent down close to hers; and in that one moment there rushed into her soul a dark, fierce hatred. Hitherto she had felt secure in his affection; now it had all vanished, and she turned, and, with feeble, tottering steps, passed down the street, her heart full of unutterable woe, and a death-like faintness stealing over her.

"Oh, if it were only death!" she cried aloud. "If I had not to live on this life of torturing anguish! He told me he loved me, and she has stolen his heart from me! She might have left me his affection. Does she—can she know that she has broken my heart?"

And all this time the thought of Lord Durant and his love that she had undervalued and cast aside never entered her mind. She never gave a moment's reflection to the fact that this was only just retribution; that she had caused a kind, trustful heart to feel the same anguish that she was now suffering. Mavis's was purely selfish grief: sympathy could find no place in her hard little heart. How she reached her lodgings Mavis never knew. It seemed like one long dream of weariness both of mind and body before she was roused by the sight of the frightened face of the landlady.

"Where have you been!" the woman

exclaimed. "I've been sitting up for you: for I was fearing you'd met with some accident, alone and on foot at this time of night: we have been half out of our senses with fright."

There was a sharpness in the woman's tone that recalled Mavis to the fact of the late hour, but she felt too miserable and worn out to make any excuses.

"Oh, Mrs. Brown!" she exclaimed, bursting into tears. "I am tired and ill: let me go to my room."

The landlady looked at her scrutinizingly for a moment, and the sight of the white, scared face roused the sympathy of her kind heart. She forbore to question her: for she could guess at part of the sad history, and Mavis could fully appreciate the kindness that she had so little expected, but it roused her to endure and bear up against the terrible blow; and the rough though well-meant endeavours to cheer her drooping spirit had the effect of calming the violence of her grief.

CHAPTER VI.

VACILLATION.

> One moment gazed—as if to gaze no more :
> Felt that for him earth held but her alone.
> Kiss'd her cold forehead—turned—and is he gone?
> BYRON.

THE morning after the ball Major Durant came into the boudoir in his mother's house, in which the ladies usually passed their mornings.

His face wore a moody, discontented expression, not at all like what would be expected of a man who only the evening before had proposed to, and been accepted by, the beautiful Isabel Ingram. He was lounging lazily back on one of the satin-covered couches, watching Mrs. Melcombe's swiftly moving knitting-pins, scarcely ever even glancing towards the impassive face of his promised bride; she sat near the window, stately and handsome as usual, with her eyes fixed on the page of the book that lay open before her.

The engagement between them had been of Mrs. Melcombe's seeking. Having no children of her own, she took a delight in settling the affairs of others; and for Isabel, whom she loved almost as a daughter, she had ever been anxious to secure a brilliant match, and had rejoiced when, that morning, the news of the fulfilment of her hopes had been declared. She had so long looked forward to it, until she never considered how a marriage with Lionel Durant must prove a ruin to Isabel's future happiness—for she knew that between them existed no affection—that it was in obedience to her wishes that Isabel had consented to barter her life for rank and wealth, which, added to her own fortune, would secure to her the position as mistress of a large establishment, which was the summit of Miss Ingram's ambition, and

Isabel was contented in the lot that she had chosen.

But it was far otherwise with Lionel; all was settled, and now, when too late, remorse and repentance came. During the past evening the gratification to his vanity in the evident preference that Isabel had shown, the not unpleasant knowledge that he was envied, had caused, for a time, forgetfulness, and he had even deceived himself into believing that his admiration for Isabel's beauty was a deeper feeling; but now, with the morning's calmer thoughts, had come recollections of Mavis and her true, unchangeable affection. How would she bear the cruel truth, the revelation that, sooner or later, must come?

"Poor little creature!" he said to himself, with a kind of contemptuous pity, "it will be a heavy trial to her, but she will get over it. I really think she does trust me, and believe in what I say; however, Mrs. Melcombe is right, I ought to marry,—it is one of the duties inseparable from riches, and Isabel will be like a queen in her own house," and as these thoughts rushed through his mind he glanced into the face whose imperial beauty had almost for a time driven Mavis's image from his heart.

"Mrs. Melcombe!" he began, abruptly, some moments after, as soon as Isabel, closing her book, had quitted the room, "I should like to fix an early date for our marriage; I am getting tired of London, and anxious to settle down in my future home."

Mrs. Melcombe looked up sharply from her work.

"This is a sudden resolve," she said, with a scrutinizing look into the major's downcast face. "I myself am no admirer of long engagements, but still I should think some delay would be preferable, in order for you to become better acquainted; besides, it is scarcely fair to Isabel. This is her first season in London; it would not do to hurry her away from all the pleasure just yet; however, of course, her wishes are the first consideration."

"No doubt they are, but cannot I persuade you to intercede for me with her?"

answered Major Durant, rising from his seat, unable to bear any longer the searching looks. "I am no longer such a very young man, and having once resolved to turn over a new leaf, and begin life afresh, all this unnecessary delay is most annoying; but I suppose they expect it, I have heard it said that the pleasantest part of a young lady's life is the time of her courtship, so I shall have to give way," he added, with a futile attempt at a smile.

Mrs. Melcombe made no reply, but Lionel's request was remembered, and she ventured to plead his cause to Isabel with an eloquence and energy that arose from her ardent desire to bring about the match.

To her surprise Isabel listened calmly and undemonstratively. "I do not see why it should not be as Major Durant wishes," she answered, looking up with some little surprise at her friend's vehemence. "I have given him my promise; he need not be afraid that I shall repent it," she added, scornfully. "You can tell him that there is no fear, but it is to be, so why need we delay?"

"Why, my dear girl, how coolly you take it! Surely you love Major Durant, when you have promised to marry him," exclaimed the elder lady.

"Love is not a necessity," answered Isabel. "It is necessary that I should marry. You would not wish me to throw myself away for a romantic fancy, like my sister has done. Major Durant neither gives nor desires love, but I am satisfied."

She rose up, and, with a stately step, moved away, to signify that she considered the interview ended, leaving Mrs. Melcombe beaming with gratification and delighted at the success with which her efforts to urge on the engagement had been rewarded.

For several days Major Durant remained at his mother's house. He appeared to be devoted in his attentions to Isabel, accompanying her in her drives and walks, even in the long shopping excursions, in which she and Mrs. Melcombe took so much interest. His engagement had altogether changed him, his mother declared triumphantly to her friend, as they watched the lovers together, apparently happy in each other's company, Isabel's face lighting up occasionally into something like animation, "I never thought that Lionel would settle down so quietly in obedience to the wishes of his friends; I never even dared to hope for the happiness that a union between Isabel and my son will bring me. He seems altogether to have outlived that one foolish action of his life. I am more thankful than I can tell that the dear girl has been sensible enough to ignore it, and to forget the wrong-doings of his past life. Her noble conduct has, no doubt, saved Lionel. Had she refused we cannot say what might have happened."

"Have you any idea what has become of that young person?" asked Mrs. Melcombe, lowering her voice almost to a whisper, and leaning forward as she spoke. "I have heard so little about the affair. Of course we never mention it at St. Hilda's.

He really did run away with her, I suppose?"

Lady Durant turned away her head to hide the troubled look on her countenance. "Do not speak of it," she said, in a husky tone, "it is more than I can bear; I am only too grateful to Isabel that she has been the means of curing him of his temporary infatuation for such an unworthy object. He has become quite a model lover, and no doubt will make an exemplary husband."

But all this devotion to Isabel only rose out of cowardice on Lionel's part. As each morning dawned he made the resolve not to delay breaking the news to Mavis of his engagement and proposed marriage, but before night came he shrank back from making the communication that would cost him so dear, and so completely blight her happiness. Time after time he sat down to write and avow the truth, but the letters were destroyed as soon as written, and thus he put off the evil day as long as possible. He carefully avoided the neighbourhood in which Mavis dwelt, dreading with an unspeakable terror the time that was so fast approaching when he must bid her farewell for ever. He loved her still; not all Isabel's charms, strive how he might, could altogether banish that bright little image from his heart, and yet the day fixed for his wedding was drawing near, and with his own lips he must break the illusion that caused Mavis to cling so lovingly to him.

"If she does not hear from me she will be sending or coming to this house," was the idea that at length dawned on his mind, and the fear of this climax had the effect of fixing his wavering resolutions, and early on the following day he set out on his way to fulfil the long-delayed duty. He had not seen Mavis for nearly three weeks; such a long absence must have caused her great uneasiness, he thought; and then he began to wonder why he had not heard of her during that time. She knew his address at his club, and yet no letter or message had arrived there.

When he approached the house the sight of a doctor's carriage before the door caused him to quicken his steps, and a terrible fear entered his mind, and bitter self-reproachful feelings were surging in his breast. In his newly aroused anxiety all other considerations were forgotten; he did not pause to think how he should make excuses for his neglect, but hurried up to the door. He was just about to raise the knocker when the door was opened and a surgeon came out, accompanied by Mrs. Brown, the landlady.

"Why, Major Durant!" exclaimed the shrill voice of the latter, "aren't you ashamed of yourself, leaving that little lady to die all alone and unhappy!"

"You don't mean to say that she's dead!" broke from Lionel's white lips, as he staggered back. "Oh, Mavis, my darling wife, has it come to this!"

"No, no, indeed, my dear sir, do not distress yourself," interposed the surgeon, advancing towards him. "Mrs. Durant is, I hope, doing well now, although it has been a hard struggle to pull her through; and the baby too seems healthy and likely to live."

"Why have I not heard of this? could

no one have sent me word?" asked Major Durant, still bewildered, but he was interrupted by the landlady's angry exclamation.

"I should like to know what you've been doing staying away all this time, leaving her to break her heart, poor little creature! Send you word indeed! it's just like you men: you fancy yourself a fine gentleman, no doubt, with your balls, concerts, and flirtations, and you just go and leave her, who cares more for you twice over than you deserve, and if you've broken her heart with your cruelty her death will lie at your door, and I don't care who hears me say it, for it's the plain truth."

"Mrs. Brown, I did not come here to be abused," answered the major, in a stern voice, which had the effect of calming the woman's vehemence. "Lead the way to Mrs. Durant's room, and announce my coming."

There was no disobeying the voice of command: the landlady slowly and unwillingly turned and preceded the major upstairs.

Mavis had heard his voice and the sound of his footsteps. She had half raised herself in bed, and with a look in which eager hope and almost terror were mingled she awaited his approach.

There was an angelic expression in her uplifted face, in the glistening eyes, with such unspeakable love shining in their depths; and yet withal the shrinking look of dread seemed to struggle with the affection that caused even his footfall to sound like music to her ears.

"Lionel, at last!" and with a choking, sobbing cry her head sank back amongst the wreathing masses of golden hair that fell over the pillows.

That morning he had been with Isabel, uttering words of constancy and love, speaking of undying affection, and trying to deceive her with empty, meaningless protestations. Now all recollections were cast to the winds, as his lips pressed those of the fair little creature to whom he had given the only affection his selfish heart had ever known. But with a cry of horror that rang through the room Mavis released herself from his embrace, and put out her hands to keep him off.

"Deceiver! traitor!" she almost shrieked. "What have I done to deserve this treatment? I trusted you; and oh, how cruelly I have been betrayed! Oh, Lionel! and I loved you so dearly!"

Her voice died into a wail of anguish that stung him more deeply than the wildest reproaches could have done. It was with a mighty effort that he could assume sufficient composure to ask in his ordinary tones,—

"What have I done?"

"Do not torture me, Lionel. I know all. I saw you with her," sobbed Mavis. "Oh, don't tell me you love her; anything would be better than that! It will break my heart! I stood in the street that night; I heard your words. Have you no pity left?"

"Hush, hush, Mavis! you are ill with excitement," interposed the major, for a moment completely taken aback by the revelation. "Do you imagine that any one could come in between us, that you can have any rival, especially in that proud, cold-hearted—"

"Be quiet, Lionel; you have no right to say that!" cried Mavis, with a wild hysterical laugh. "You cannot deceive me. I have seen it in the papers that Isabel Ingram is your promised wife."

"Curse the papers!" thundered forth Major Durant. "You mustn't believe anything, Mavis, except that, whatever comes, I shall ever remain true to you. You must know as well as I do that it would have been ruin to me if I had obeyed my heart's desire. It is a duty I owe to society to marry Isabel; but I am not bound to love her."

"This is only making it harder, Lionel!" answered Mavis, striving to speak calmly. "I have known my dreadful fate long enough to realize it a little now; perhaps I deserve it all. This is our last meeting, and before we part you must promise to forget—" She was about to add more; but the effort was too great, and, covering her face, she sobbed in heart-broken silence.

"I cannot forget you, my only love, my angel! I will give up all for you. What do I care what the world says!" began Lionel, vehemently; but Mavis stopped him.

"No, my mind is made up," she answered, in broken sentences, between her sobs. "If you could have forgotten me enough to pledge your word to another we had better part. No one shall say that Mavis Durant proved a drawback and a disgrace to the man she trusted. I have my child, and she is more than I deserve."

"Our child," corrected the major, in a low voice, full of real repentance for the cruel part he had played, but feeling all the while that Mavis was right, and it was incumbent on them that they should separate. "Let me see her, and oh, how can I forgive myself for blighting your existence, and that of an innocent child!"

"You should have thought of that before," sorrowfully responded Mavis. "It is too late now; you cannot make reparation for the wrong you have done us both."

She turned round as she uttered these

words, and showed him the face of the sleeping infant; a fair little creature with tiny rings of golden hair clustering on its head, even at that tender age already showing promises of future loveliness.

"She was born last Tuesday week," continued Mavis, eagerly watching the expression on Lionel's face as he bent forward to look at his child.

"I think I can trace a likeness to you, Mavis," he said, huskily, turning away his head and moving to the other side of the room, unable any longer to meet her glance. "Oh, Mavis, are we to part for ever? Will you drive me away like this?" he resumed. "How can I ever know happiness apart from you!"

"Do you imagine that this parting costs me nothing? Cannot you realize what I have endured to bring me to this resolve?" she asked, starting up with a piteous look of appeal. "Let us not prolong this interview. Each moment makes it worse to bear. Go away now; your duty to your future wife demands you!"

"My duty to my future wife keeps me here!" he replied, advancing again to the bedside and taking her in his arms. "Mavis, believe me, I am speaking the truth now, I shall marry no one but you, who have been true to me through so much. I can see in your eyes that you can no longer resist my entreaty. Say you still love me; do not drive me into misery."

"But Miss Ingram — what of your promises to her!" faltered Mavis.

"Are my promises to her to be regarded before your happiness? She knows I never cared for her, she will get over it directly. There, now, I see all hesitation has gone, and you consent. What do I care about the opinions of the world? If my mother does not choose to receive as a daughter the only woman who ever shall be my wife, she must leave it alone; we can be happy in each other's society, cannot we, my darling? I shall go this very day and make arrangements for our marriage to take place as soon as you have recovered your health."

Mavis made no reply; Lionel's pleading

and her own affectionate nature had done its work. She could no longer keep up the fierce struggle of opposition, but lay back amongst the pillows, listening with a peaceful smile as he spoke of the future; and there was a great joy in her heart, produced by this sudden transition from despair to hope.

Soon, however, the first reckless feelings that had driven all but the image of Mavis from his heart began to give place to serious consideration, and a look of deep perplexity darkened Major Durant's brow. It would be almost ruin to him, and yet it must be done, and Isabel must be informed that she could never be his wife. Already he foresaw opposition and difficulties, that almost made him repent of the weakness that had caused him to pledge his word to Mavis. Her voice was the first to break the silence that had fallen on them both; it sounded strangely altered since she had last spoken.

"Lionel, Lady Durant must know of this. How shall you tell her? Have you strength of mind sufficient to bear the ordeal of her disapproval?" she asked, quietly raising her eyes and looking full into his downcast, gloomy face.

"I hope so!" he answered, with an effort. "I must hasten away; and in one short hour I shall return, never more to leave you until death! How could I have been so faithless, so base, as to forsake you as I have done! Can you ever fully forgive me? But now I am firmly fixed in my resolve. Good-bye, dearest, until I return."

He was gone in a moment; without another glance at the face that was beaming with the newly aroused, intense happiness.

He walked slowly along; for his mind was full of dark forebodings. The more he tried to consider, the more confused seemed the entanglement into which he had allowed himself to be drawn; but as each step brought him nearer to his mother's house, a kind of defiant recklessness took possession of him, and he resolved to face the evil boldly and without hesitation to declare his intentions.

There were visitors in the drawing-room when he came in, and it was with difficulty that he managed to nerve himself sufficiently to enter into conversation with them. He had a vague consciousness of Isabel's presence; he felt her eyes fixed on him—that she detected something strange in his manner, but no suspicion of the truth dawned in her mind, or revealed itself in her self-possessed stateliness.

The departure of the visitors was followed by the announcement of luncheon, and Isabel quitted the room to obey the summons. Lady Durant was about to follow her when her son placed himself before her.

"Mother, one word with you alone!" he cried; and the look he gave her caused an exclamation of alarm to rise to her lips.

"Lionel, what has happened?" she asked.

He made no immediate reply, but, leading her back into the room, closed the door.

"Now I may speak. It is not too late to declare it, I cannot marry Isabel."

"What do you mean, Lionel! Not marry Isabel! Do you know what you are saying?

The wedding-day is fixed; everything is arranged, and you declare that you will draw back. It cannot be; it is too late now!"

"I know it all, and how weak and cowardly I have been; but I again declare it is not too late. How can I marry, when my heart is given to another?" he answered, speaking rapidly in his vehemence. "I ought to have known that I have loved once and for always; and the only one being to whom I can ever give my whole affection is Mavis."

He paused, with his arms folded; and for once there was an elevated look that gave a new beauty to his countenance.

In speechless dismay Lady Durant sank back on to a seat, and covered her face with her hands, as if to shut out the terrible vision that his words had produced. He had expected reproaches and anger, and he could have borne them bravely, knowing that it was no more than he deserved; but, as it was, to behold instead the crushed, hopeless look of despair and anguish, all the arguments with which he had steeled himself were scattered to the winds.

"You know it was only to please you that I was drawn into an engagement with Isabel," continued Major Durant. "I never considered what it would cost me. Now that I have discovered what my real feelings are I shall go openly and demand a release from the engagement."

"And you wish to marry that girl Mavis! Lionel, why is it that she should for ever come in between you and your mother's love? For thirty years you have been the idol of my existence, and now you will cast aside all the affection I have lavished on you, for the sake of an unworthy creature like she is. Can you compare her selfish admiration of you with my love and devotion?"

"Never for one moment!" answered the major, vehemently. "My love for her could never make me forget your self-sacrifice; but will not the affection of a husband and father cause me more fully to appreciate your love for me?"

"No, no, it cannot!" Lady Durant almost

shrieked. "You will have to choose between her and me. Once married to her, and for ever we must separate! Lionel, it will kill me if you thus disgrace yourself; besides, your word to Isabel—you have pledged it!"

"I do not forget that," he replied, quietly and sorrowfully, approaching nearer to his mother, who still sat motionless, with the same despairing expression. "But will that bear comparison with the duty that so plainly lies before me?"

"You have but one path of duty, and that I need not point out to you," said Lady Durant. "You know it already. By a marriage with Isabel you will triumph over the fearfully foolish act in your life, and regain the position in society that you would madly throw aside for ever. For my sake consider before you act so rashly, and tell me what has happened to cause you thus suddenly to come to this fatal determination."

"I have seen Mavis this morning," replied Major Durant. "The sight of her and her child brought me to the knowledge of the only honourable course open to me. You will surely not continue your opposition, against which I dare not attempt to combat?"

A fierce struggle between duty and inclination, produced by his mother's words, was taking place in Major Durant's mind. A marriage with Isabel meant a brilliant future in the eyes of the world—very tempting to the man who had so sorely chafed against his temporary isolation from society. With Mavis there would be obscurity, with the over-present blight on his reputation that could not be removed; and would affection be sufficient to compensate for all these drawbacks?"

"What am I to do?" he exclaimed, at length, in desperation. "In either case the future seems dark and hopeless. How can I live with the torturing knowledge of my cruelty in deserting one to whom I am bound by the ties of honour and duty? You surely do not urge me to act so basely? Think of her feelings, for she loves me far better than I deserve!"

Lady Durant rose from her seat and moved towards the door.

"It is useless to prolong this painful discussion," she said, striving to appear outwardly calm. "Oh, that I had never lived to see this day!—that I had died before my son brought this extra disgrace upon himself! Is there no hope that you can save yourself from this sacrifice? Only think over it, and come to a right determination!"

The appealing look she gave him touched Lionel's heart. He sprang forward to detain her, as she was leaving the room.

"You give me no alternative!" he said, in a low voice. "Poor Mavis, it will break her heart. How can I tell her of my faithlessness!"

He seemed unable to utter another word, but turned away from his mother. However, Lady Durant knew that she had conquered, and that was sufficient for her. She made no attempt to renew the conversation, but stood where she was, silently regarding him, wondering in her own mind how great the struggle was that he had undergone.

"Are you coming in to luncheon, Lady Durant?" asked Isabel, entering the room. At that moment Lionel glanced up at the sound of the gentle, lady-like voice, and met the gaze of the proud dark eyes.

"It is my fate," he said to himself. "How could I even for a moment be so blind to Isabel's superior charms, and so rash as to run the risk of ruining all my prospects in life?"

During the remainder of the day Major Durant appeared to have forgotten the passionate declaration of constancy that he had uttered that morning. Even his mother, accustomed as she had been to conceal her feelings, wondered at and admired his self-control, as she watched him conversing with Isabel or the other visitors who were staying in the house, with rather more than his usual gaiety of manner.

But if she had seen him a few hours later, seated at his desk, writing the letter that was destined for ever to separate Mavis from him—the few words which, strive how he might, he could not soften, or make the heavy, bitter blow fall less painfully on the loving heart that he felt he was breaking—if Lady Durant had seen him, with his head bent down on to his folded arms, with the finished letter lying before him, she would then have known how his apparent light-heartedness had been but a mask to conceal his real feelings; and that even then, when his resolve was fixed, he still felt deep regrets for that which might have been—even she must have felt pity for him.

"This is only cowardice!" he exclaimed at last. "I must not give way like this!" And when the door was suddenly opened, he slipped the envelope into his pocket, fearing lest the address should be observed.

It was Mrs. Melcombe who entered. Her sharp, inquiring eyes wandered round the room, seeming to take in all at a glance, and almost (so Major Durant could not help imagining) to be able to read the thoughts expressed on his troubled countenance.

"You promised to drive out with us this

afternoon," she said, as the major hastily thrust into his desk several torn sheets of paper, on which he had begun the letter, and then thrown aside, half inclined to give up the distasteful, self-imposed duty. " It will disappoint Isabel if you do not accompany her," she continued. " However, I suppose you are better employed."

"No, indeed!" answered Major Durant, quickly. "I shall be ready in half a minute, when I have finished my letters. Ask Isabel to wait for me."

It was too late now. Even if the major had felt inclined, he could not recall that letter, as with trembling, nervous fingers he slipped it into the pillar-post opposite to his mother's house, and then turned and took his seat with Isabel and Mrs. Melcombe in the carriage.

"Why did you not give your letter to Stevens to post?" asked Mrs. Melcombe, as they drove off. "It must be most important to induce you to soil your boots on the muddy road, instead of sending a servant," she added, sarcastically.

Lionel laughed uneasily. "I prefer to post my letters myself," he answered. "Then, if a mistake occurs, I alone am to blame."

"I suppose it is to your brother. I observed the name of Durant on the address," resumed Mrs. Melcombe. "I was not aware you corresponded with him. Is there a chance that we shall have him at the wedding?"

"No, I do not think he will come," replied the major, suddenly becoming interested in a passing conveyance, which he appeared to be eagerly looking after. But the heightened colour and confused manner did not escape Mrs. Melcombe's observant eyes, although Isabel remained calm and statuesque as ever.

CHAPTER VII.

HE COMETH NOT, SHE SAID.

Nay, doubt me not, though all thy love hath ceased—
I know it hath—yet, yet believe, at least,
That every spark of reason's light must be
Quench'd in this brain ere I could part from thee!
MOORE.

MAJOR DURANT's anxiety to quit London grew greater as the 9th of June, the day appointed for his wedding, approached. Once away from the place where Mavis dwelt, he told himself, he could again feel free from the recollection of his faithlessness to her. He had not heard from or seen her since he had written to declare his marriage with her impossible. He comforted himself with the assurance of his mother's declaration that she would soon get over it, and the knowledge that he was acting according to the wishes of his friends was sufficient to produce a feeling of self-satisfaction.

At length the day arrived; the ceremony was concluded, and the bride and bridegroom started on their Continental tour with every outward show of gaiety and happiness, and in all the fashionable crowd of guests assembled at the church, and breakfast that followed, there was not one to give a thought to the poor forlorn woman, who, in a far distant part of the bustling, crowded city, was lying at that time ill in mind and body, hovering between life and death, and longing only for an end to her sufferings.

It was with skill and tenderness that the kind-hearted landlady nursed Mavis back to life. She knew all the sad history. The delirious ravings had informed her of Major Durant's desertion of her, and she could only feel pity for one who had loved as Mavis had done.

"But you must try and live for your child's sake; she needs your care doubly now," were the words that first roused the drooping spirits to the necessity of exertion, and Mavis knew that to live she must work. Lionel had offered her money; a handsome income, sufficient to support her with every comfort, was at her disposal, but could she take it? No; it was impossible. Her child should never be dependent on the money with which Major Durant had vainly imagined he could compensate her for having blighted her life.

The bright, hot summer weather had given place to autumn, and the London season had long been over, before Mavis was able calmly to consider the future, and to think over the means of earning her livelihood. From the newspapers she found out that Major Durant and Isabel had returned to England, and had taken up their abode at the country house that Lionel had purchased in Sussex. Mavis could read his name coupled with Isabel's calmly now, without the great pain at her heart that she had felt when she had heard the news of the wedding. Time had softened the blow, and she could even spare a thought of pity for Isabel, and a hope that she would never know the true character of the man she had married.

"I am sure I try not to feel unkindly towards her," she said to herself, as she laid the newspaper down, "but it is hard to think altogether charitably of one who has come in between us, and taken all his affection from me. Had it not been for her, I might have known happiness instead of life-long remorse and degradation."

The return of the painful thoughts that anxiety for her child's future had for a time served to banish was interrupted by the entrance of the landlady with the weekly bill, the sight of which Mavis was learning to dread. Real poverty had been hitherto an unknown evil; even when she had formerly earned her living she had always had friends to recommend and help her; now all was changed, for how could she hope to return to her old profession, which seemed the only means of gaining a livelihood? Many and many a sleepless night had she passed pondering over her dark lot, and often bitter tears of remorse fell as she contemplated the baby, to whom she could only give an inheritance of shame. She looked up appealingly as the landlady came in and seated herself opposite to her.

"I wish you could try and settle what's owing," she began. "You see I don't want to be hard, but I've got my own children to think of."

Mavis started from her seat with a cry of pain.

"Oh, Mrs. Brown, what will become of us if I cannot find something to do! I have tried again and again, but only to meet with disappointment, and now almost all my money is gone. I wonder if there ever was any one so utterly miserable as I am!"

"It's foolish to fret like that; the best thing you can do is to look on hopefully; happier times must come," was the answer. "Come, cheer up. I can't bear to see you always crying. I'm sure if you are hard up for money I'll try and make shift a little longer, though my rent's due, and my landlord's a sharp man."

Mavis slowly drew out her purse, and counted out the remainder of the small stock of coins.

"This is all I have, Mrs. Brown," she said. "When it is gone I must leave here; I cannot live on in your debt, although it will grieve me sorely. You are the only friend I have." As she uttered these words she bent down, and took her baby from its cradle; her tears were falling fast on its fair little face. "I do not care what I do, but you must not come to want, my darling!" she exclaimed, and then, looking up suddenly, she resumed, "do you think you could obtain music pupils for me? I do not care how little they pay so that I could earn something. My voice ought to be as good as ever it was, if only I could afford the hire of a piano."

Mrs. Brown promised to do her best, and by speaking to her friends and representing Mavis as a young widow lady she managed to obtain four little girls, to whom she gave instruction twice a week. It was but a small sum that she was able to earn, and teaching was hard drudgery; but still it was a commencement, and it might lead to something more.

She was obliged to leave her comfortable rooms. Mrs. Brown found other lodgers who could better afford to pay the rather high rent, and now she occupied a large, poorly furnished room at the top of the house.

It was there that the first years of infancy were spent by little Dolores; for that was the name that Mavis had given during her illness, when they had asked her wishes concerning her child's name.

"Shall we call her Mavis?" Mrs. Brown asked, but the heart-broken young mother had shaken her head. "No, not that; she must not bear my name, it can only prove a curse to her. Call her Dolores."

And so the child had been called Dolores —and in the bare room, often chilly and cold in winter, with the draught coming in through the badly fitting window that looked over the roofs of the other houses—she first learned to take notice of what was going on round her, and to receive the whole share of her mother's idolizing affection. But she did not seem to return it. There never was a response to the fond terms of endearment; never a look of affection in the large, pale-blue eyes that were always opened widely, and fixed with a meaningless gaze on her mother's face, at the age when most children begin to return with some love all the care lavished on them.

Occasionally the lovely face was distorted with passion, and with her small, beautifully formed arms and hands she would strike her mother in paroxysms of ungovernable rage that alarmed Mavis by their frequent recurrence.

"It is because I am obliged to leave her so much, poor little thing; she gets neglected," explained Mavis, when Mrs. Brown came to her one day to complain of the child.

Dolores was then nearly three years of age; a tall, healthy child, able to find her way by herself about the large house, and sometimes in Mavis's absence it taxed the landlady's patience to keep the little one out of danger and harm.

"If she were my child I'd give her a good whipping!" was the angry answer. "Naughty little thing, she seems to take delight in breaking everything she lays her hands on."

There was one thing that Mavis could not bear, and that was to hear her child blamed, and this was the commencement of her first disagreement with the landlady. In her indignation she made the resolve that, whatever happened, Dolores must not be left so much to the care of strangers, and yet what could she do? All the lessons she gave were at her pupils' own residences. Teaching occupied her during the greater part of the day, for her fine voice had been the means of causing her to be sought after as a singing-mistress; hitherto she had shrunk from the publicity of reappearing before the public. But, having become suddenly aroused to the fact of the injurious effect this mode of life was having on her child's mind, all these scruples disappeared, and Mavis managed to obtain an engagement at a small theatre. It was easier work than teaching; her voice had improved and strengthened, and before long she was able to earn sufficient to afford to return to her old rooms, and engage a servant to attend on Dolores.

And thus she passed through the first bitter struggle with poverty, and for a time brighter days began to dawn for Mavis. Her spirits rose from the state of melancholy suffering that the long period of adverse fate had produced. Almost every night she sang before crowded audiences, her fresh pure voice rang out as sweetly as in the old days, before she had known or dreamt of the wild unrest of life that she had undergone. Under the assumed name of Danvers, by which she was now known, she felt secure from recognition. She was beginning partially to outlive the past, and even sometimes a longing came over her to return to the happier life she had quitted.

Had she forgotten her love?

CHAPTER VIII.

ON THE BEACH.

> He heeds them not: one smile of hers
> Is worth a world of worshippers;
> They but the star's adorers are,
> She is the heaven that lights the star!
> MOORE.

THE sea was very calm, scarcely a ripple appeared; the waves seemed to steal up sullenly, just a slight rolling motion beneath the surface, before they broke, with a prolonged roar, on the stony beach at Pen Vychan.

The sky was intensely blue, with the deep colour so rarely seen in this cold climate of ours, but the fleecy white clouds drifting along betokened, in spite of the treacherous smoothness of the water, that rough weather was at hand. Coming down on to the beach, after a long, hot walk through the valley, Jessie Williams slackened her pace, and stood for a few minutes to enjoy the cool evening breeze, that was so pleasant. The sun was setting like a large globe of crimson fire; the horizon shone brightly with gorgeous tints of red and golden light. Each little feathery cloud soon became flecked with brightness; and far away, in the north, the ponderous storm-clouds, that showed themselves above the horizon, glowed like the hidden fire from a furnace, and with brilliant flashing glory the sparkling billows reflected the light, throwing it around until earth, sky, and sea were all blended together in a luminous panorama of brightness. She remained motionless, entranced with the sight which she had so often beheld, but each time it presented a new beauty to her eyes.

Straight in the path of light she stood; the ruddy glare falling on her quiet, thoughtful face, that seemed just then to have gained a new beauty. She looked absolutely pretty, in her dark, well-fitting dress and broad-brimmed, shady hat; there was a quiet, lady-like grace about her, an innate refinement of appearance and manner that had not altogether been acquired in her native village. So thought a tall, fine-looking young man, whose dark hair and bronzed complexion revealed that he had long dwelt in foreign countries. He walked swiftly, with a firm, resolute step, that in itself betokened energy and strength of character, even had it not been for the noble broad brow and earnest dark eyes beaming with the fire of genius.

Within a few paces of the silent little figure he stopped; she heard his footstep on the shingle, and turned her head.

"Jessie!" he cried.

"Ivor, is that you?"

And thus the lovers met, after long years of separation, that had been spent by Ivor first at the university; and then, after returning to St. Hilda's for a short period, he went abroad, and passed some years in travelling about, visiting many climes that he had so often longed to behold.

"I have come at length to claim you, dearest!" said Ivor, as they left the shore, and pursued their way along the village streets. "Do you remember that time when I declared I should return rich and famous, to demand a fulfilment of your promise? I have not been able to accomplish the last part of my compact: fate has decreed it otherwise. It was not destined that I should pursue the career I once hoped for, but need that make any difference? Jessie, I have seen your father, and gained the permission that he withheld when I had the audacity to ask it before."

Jessie's answer was soon given. She had never forgotten Ivor's love all through the years that Lord Durant had thought fit to separate them.

Ivor was too young to know his own mind, the nobleman had declared, and he would not allow him to bind himself to an engagement that might prove a drawback to him. However, the young man had remained true to his first and only love; he had met in society many fashionable, fascinating young ladies, far beyond Jessie Williams in rank and beauty, but he had not felt the power of their charms; through all he was steadfast: and so Lord Durant had no longer withheld his sanction; he had permitted his son to depart for Pen Vychan, and with his own lips speak the words that would send joy into the true heart that was waiting for him. It took a long time before they reached Mr. Williams's house; there was so much to be talked about, so many adventures to be related, and scenes to be described, that it was quite dark before they entered the shabby little parlour, looking shabbier and more dingy than ever.

"And now I have talked enough about myself," said Ivor, as they seated themselves together on the old horsehair-covered sofa. "I must know about you; what have you been doing all this time?"

"There is so little to relate," replied Jessie, simply. "I stayed on at St. Hilda's for nearly six months after you went to

Cambridge. Then my sister Gwendoline's marriage and my poor mother's illness rendered it necessary that I should return home. After my mother's death I could not go back, for my father wanted me to take care of the house, and so I have been here ever since, leading the same quiet life that you know so well, and trying to cheer my father, for our great trouble altered him terribly. Do you not think he is changed?"

"Yes, he looks old and worn; I am afraid the work in this large parish is too hard for him," answered Ivor. "When I take you away to St. Hilda's could not you persuade him to accompany us?"

"Oh, no, indeed; I am sure he will never leave Pen Vychan," interrupted Jessie. "It would half break his heart to give up the parish in which he has worked for so long. He would be wretched without anything to do."

"He need not lead an idle life in St. Hilda's," gravely answered Ivor. "There is plenty of work there even yet, in spite of my father's struggles to improve the place, which have only been partially successful. However, I will consult him about it before we say any more."

They were interrupted by the entrance of Mr. Williams, and presently they sat down to partake of tea. It was a simply served meal, and it seemed strange to Ivor to look back through what seemed to him a long vista of years to the time when the privilege of sitting at that same table had been an almost unheard-of favour, when he had only dared to worship Jessie from a distance, only in his day-dreams venturing even to hope to be ultimately able to win her: now he was admitted as a welcome visitor by Mr. Williams, who regarded it as an honour that the nobleman's heir should ask his daughter's hand in marriage. During the course of the evening he even caught himself smiling at the change that altered circumstances will bring.

A few days were spent very happily in the old village, accompanying Jessie about in her walks and visits of charity to the very cottages where he had formerly been received as a friend and equal.

"How very thankful and grateful I ought to be to you, my darling, for having ignored my humble bringing up! Should I ever have known this happiness if you had been cold and proud, and disdained the love of a poor artist?" asked Ivor, as they lingered together for the last leave-taking, when the day had arrived for him to go back to St. Hilda's, not to return again until the day before the wedding, about which all had been settled.

Jessie looked up with a bright, happy smile. "I could not help showing what I felt, Ivor," she replied. "I trusted in your genius, and knew that even if good fortune had not befallen you it would have gained renown."

There was very little more to be said, for the sound of the coach could be heard approaching, and there was a tender, loving leave-taking; and a moment after Jessie stood gazing after the vehicle, until a turn in the road hid them from each other's sight.

Ivor was inexpressibly happy, with only

one cloud on the bright horizon of the future—the temporary parting with Jessie. But it was to be for so short a time, only sufficient for the preparations for the wedding to be completed, before he would see her again. And surely, after the long time he had been away from his father, it was not his duty to grudge the few short weeks that Lord Durant wished to spend in his son's society.

The Abbey appeared very dreary and desolate to Ivor, coming, as he did, from the pure air and freshness of Pen Vychan. And it was with a feeling of weariness and almost discontent that as soon as he arrived at home he went into the gloomy library.

There was something oppressive to his artistic nature in the melancholy aspect and the cheerless look of the smoke-stained evergreens that grew close up to the windows; with the recollection fresh in his mind of the walks taken with Jessie through the fair valleys of his native village, or by the sea, the very sight and sound of which he loved so well.

But in an instant the thought was dismissed. If St. Hilda's seemed desolate and unlovely to him, whose future was destined to be one of happiness, what must it be to his father, to whom Pen Vychan had been for so many years a peaceful, self-chosen home? But *he* had given up all; and with nothing to look forward to, no ray of light to fall across the dark path of his existence, he had devoted his life to the benefit of others.

The entrance of a servant with a letter put an end to his musings.

"It came for you, sir, by this morning's post," said the man, handing it to his young master.

"Thank you. Has my father come in?" asked Ivor, tearing open the envelope, and glancing over the contents with an eager, hurried look.

"No, sir," was the reply. "His lordship left word that if you came in first, I was to say he would be in by dinner-time."

"Very well," said Ivor, turning again to the perusal of the letter; and the footman, waiting a moment to see if there were any further orders, noiselessly vanished from the room.

It was with an expression of surprise that Ivor at length laid down the letter, after having carefully read it through.

It was from his mother, and ran thus,—

"My DEAR SON,—Perhaps you will be surprised to receive this letter from one who has so completely given up correspondence with the outer world. It is only the fact of receiving such constant news from you that induces me to reply to it; for hard as I struggle against the feeling, I cannot forget the few brief weeks we spent together, when, without knowing of the close tie of relationship between us, I felt my heart drawn towards you as it never was before to any living being.

"Your descriptions of the life you have been leading since we parted have roused me to fresh exertions. Beneath this sunny southern sky I fear I am becoming too selfish, too fond of ease, and am acquiring a disinclination for hard, active work.

"You spoke of London in your last letter, and of one who is in that city, struggling against poverty, to which her own wrong-doing has led her. I remember it well—that time when I beheld the look of horror pass over that lovely young creature's face, when she was told (with the cruel deceit in which Lionel Durant is an adept) that Lord Durant was not her husband.

"At that time I pitied the young girl: I can scarcely do so now, although I hardly dare even write these words; for has my life been sinless? have not I wronged Lord Durant more cruelly than I can bear to think of?

"It is to try in some measure to make reparation for my past conduct that I purpose returning to England, and, taking up my abode in London, endeavour to find means of doing good there.

"For your father's sake, Ivor, I shall seek out that erring woman, and if it is possible try to be of some benefit to her. I shall watch over her, and depend upon it, the time will soon come for me to try and show my repentance by my care of the only woman Gerald Durant ever truly loved.

"I intend to leave Rome in a few days, and shall be in London before this month is over. You may tell Sybil Monticth of my resolve, for I should like to see her again: but on no account must you mention it to your father. I would not have him know the reason that induces me to quit the home that I had hoped would be mine through life. I rely on you as long as the remembrance of his love remains not to mention my name to him. I would rather he should forget that there was still living such a person as

"Your loving mother,
"Veronica."

A sigh escaped Ivor's lips as he read to the end, and his eyes were dimmed with moisture when he laid the letter down.

"How noble and self-denying she is!" he said to himself, "and yet so anxious that her goodness should remain unknown. Oh, if I only could tell my father!—even he must honour her for this. I must write to Jessie, and tell her, for she must learn to know and love my mother."

He smiled as he repeated the last words. Hitherto Sister Veronica had resisted all his entreaties to receive him as her son, and, until now, had never even alluded to the relationship.

"If she had only signed her true name," he thought, "it would have seemed more like giving up the life of voluntary banishment; but she appears as determined as ever to abide by her resolutions. Still I shall not give up hope; perhaps some day my wish may be accomplished, and my father and mother may be induced to forgive each other."

Meanwhile Lord Durant was seated in the large airy studio built on at the back of the small house which Claude Montieth and his wife had occupied since their return from Italy. The artist was busy at his easel over the painting at which he was obliged to work, but, like all its predecessors, it would be sure to meet with a ready sale.

Although still pale and delicate-looking, his face had regained a look of health which had not been there until Lord Durant's patronage had created a fashion for his paintings; still he had sometimes to work almost beyond his strength to provide for the two rosy-cheeked little boys, who had come up on Lord Durant's entrance to hear the wonderful tales that he so often found time to relate to them.

The youngest of the family, a daughter, lay in Sybil's arms—a snow-white little creature, whom the proud young mother had brought downstairs to display to the nobleman.

The sound of the clock striking the hour of six caused Lord Durant to break off suddenly in the midst of his conversation with Sybil.

"I really must not remain any longer, Mrs. Montieth. I shall so soon lose Ivor altogether," he said, "that I cannot afford to stay away from him all evening, on the first day of his return."

As Lord Durant uttered these words Sybil looked up to him with a merry smile.

"I understood that Ivor was still going to reside at the Abbey after his marriage?" said the artist, putting the question that Sybil was about to utter.

"Yes, and so he is," was the nobleman's reply; "but I fear I shall not see much of him. I cannot expect his young bride to care for the society of a morose old man like I am. Of course my son is bound to me by ties of duty and gratitude, but I should not think he could feel much real natural affection."

"I am certain you misjudge Ivor," interrupted Sybil, with some indignation. "If you blame him for spending so much time in travelling, he believed it was your wish; and if you think of the wonderful improvement in him I am sure you ought to feel satisfied."

"And so I am satisfied, more satisfied and thankful than I know how to express," said Lord Durant, in a tone of deep feeling. "Who would have imagined that a lad brought up amongst ignorant seamen, and surrounded by temptations as he was, would have raised himself as Ivor has done? I need never feel ashamed now of allowing him to associate with gentlemen of any rank. Had it not been for the one drawback, I should be wholly and completely proud of my son : it is a disappointment that he should choose to marry into *that* family."

He alluded to the relationship of Jessie to Mavis, and a silence fell on his hearers. He never spoke of her by name, and only the few who knew Lord Durant intimately were aware of the continual silent suffering that he still bore, keeping it, however, to himself, not allowing his own troubles to rob him of sympathy or care for others; and yet a smile rarely was seen on that grave face, now lined and altered with a look of age far beyond his years.

He soon rose to take leave, and passed down the busy, bustling streets, receiving many a pleasant greeting from the passers-by, and stopping once or twice on his way to speak to some humbly-clad working man or woman.

"How do you do, Lord Durant? it is

quite an age since I have seen you." In turning the corner of the street he came face to face with Mrs. Melcombe, advancing towards him, holding out her hand and smiling graciously. He would fain have passed her, but she prevented him, so that to avoid stopping without rudeness was impossible. She began by expressing her congratulations on Ivor's approaching marriage. "It will be such a comfort to you to have a daughter at the Abbey," she continued, "and to know that your son will remain more at home. I will call to see him, if I can, one of these days, for I hear he has returned this afternoon; but my time is really so much taken up that I scarcely have a moment to call my own, and Isabel is coming to visit me shortly. I am sure the dear girl needs a change after all her troubles; it will be quite a relief to her to have the comfort of my sympathy. Ah, men are sad creatures, and if I had known what I do now I should have striven hard to prevent the match."

Her sharp, inquisitive eyes were fixed on

Lord Durant's face, and, though he was striving to keep down the emotion that the allusion to his brother's marriage had brought, he could not prevent the spasm of pain that passed across his features.

"Of course you would be the last to hear, not being friendly with the major," Mrs. Melcombe went on to say, "but poor Isabel's letters are filled with heartrending descriptions of what she has to endure from her husband."

"The affairs of Major Durant and his wife do not interest me, Mrs. Melcombe," coldly replied the nobleman: "you must please to allow me to proceed on my way."

He raised his hat to her, and was gone in a moment, leaving Mrs. Melcombe disgusted and angry.

"He need not have taken offence so easily," she said to herself, looking after Lord Durant's retreating figure. "Surely before this he must have grown accustomed to the mention of his brother's name. He sets himself up for being more charitable than his neighbours, and yet he cannot spare a word of sympathy for Isabel, the poor ill-used wife."

Mrs. Melcombe's words had revived thoughts in Lord Durant's heart that for five years he had been striving to conquer. He still cherished the memory of his love for Mavis with a kind of pitying tenderness; the first keen sharpness of grief was subdued; she was dead to him, and he tried to think of her kindly and gently, as if she had really passed away from the world. He had long discovered that it was impossible to forget, and now the recollection had come to him of how equally impossible it was to forgive the wrong his brother had done him.

"And so he is unhappy with his wife, and the knowledge of this brings a thought of satisfaction. Is this a right feeling?" he asked himself, slackening his pace, and pursuing his way slowly beneath the shadow of his own trees: "ought I not rather to feel sorrow for one who is in the power of that man who stole away my life's happiness? Could it have been ambition that made her marry him? for she must have known what he was!"

Ivor was strolling up and down in front of the house, and as Lord Durant caught sight of his son he strove to shake off the melancholy that was stealing into his heart; he rarely revealed his feelings to others, and he did not wish that his son should receive a gloomy welcome home again.

They stayed talking together for a few moments, and then the nobleman ascended the steps, and, crossing the hall, went into the library. There he met with a smile of welcome from one who always felt for him, and appeared to understand and appreciate his thoughts. It was little Maud Austin. It was, perhaps, the striking likeness to Mavis in her young sister that drew the hearts of the old man and the child so closely together, or else the knowledge that she was the only being in the world who gave him true, unselfish affection, but to Maud he would speak on subjects that rarely passed his lips. She never found him incomprehensible or morose, as so many people declared he was, and when she heard herself pitied for the isolated life to which her lameness condemned her, and Lord Durant was recommended to send her to school, where she would meet with companionship, she declared her determination of never leaving him; she knew how he cared for her society, and how she was able to keep him from the despair of utter loneliness.

"When Ivor is married I shall miss my little companion," said Lord Durant, as the child drew up a low stool, and took her favourite seat beside him. "Jessie will be your chief friend then; you used to be so fond of her."

Maud shook her head.

"No, Jessie will have Ivor," she replied. "I shall be more with you than ever. Do you think I shall ever love any one as much as you, who are so very kind, when there is no one else who cares for me in the whole world? I have often wondered what makes you so very good to me."

"Don't you know, Maud?" asked the nobleman, fondly stroking the curly golden hair, and looking down into the thoughtful blue eyes that were so like her sister's; he could hardly realize that she was still a child, there was such a grave, womanly expression in the pretty face. It grew suddenly saddened, as she answered in a low voice,—

"I think I do; am I really so very much like my sister? I can remember when I used to think her so good and lovely; I wish she would come back again."

"I wonder where she is now! Oh that there were some means of knowing or hearing the tidings for which my heart longs so sorely!" continued Lord Durant, in a dreamy, subdued tone, uttering aloud the thoughts that were passing through his mind.

"Ivor says he believes she is in London. She is a singer," replied Maud, quietly.

"So near, and yet parted further than if oceans divided us! Oh, Mavis, my heart's treasure, if you only knew what you had cost me!" murmured the nobleman, and then he remained quiet and still, as if he could behold in a vision the happiness that was denied him; and Maud would not disturb or break in on the sad, silent reverie.

CHAPTER IX.

DOLORES.

> But then it had its mother's eyes,
> And they were all to love and me.
>
> Byron.

"Isabel, I've a good mind to go with you; there is nothing to be done here at this season. Every one has gone away to the sea-coast, and the shooting has not begun yet."

"I thought you hated St. Hilda's," answered Isabel Durant to her husband's observations, without raising her eyes from her book.

"So I do, but one place is as unbearable as another, owing to your obstinate refusal to go to Ireland with me," was her husband's retort.

"Lionel, I've told you before that nothing will induce me to cross the sea again; however, you can go alone; I do not care, I'm sure. We poor wives get used to neglect. I dare say I can find my way to Mrs. Melcombe's without your escort, if you have no objection to my visiting my own friends," Isabel continued, with an air of irritating humility.

"The other day you were complaining of how much I left you. Now, when I propose to accompany you to Mrs. Melcombe's, you turn round. How am I to understand a woman's wishes?" asked Major Durant, rather angrily.

"Oh, please yourself. I do not wish to urge you against your own will. Of course if you care to run the risk of meeting Lord Durant you may go and welcome."

"I'm not afraid of Gerald. I am no more likely to encounter him than you are to meet your sister, Mrs. Montieth. I suppose if you meet in the street you will not speak to her, after the terrible disgrace she brought on the family?" asked Lionel, with a grim smile of satisfaction.

"I do not know that I should. I am beginning to think Sybil did not act so unwisely after all. She, at least, married a man who cared for her, and not only for his own selfish gratification," cried Isabel. "I'm sure I envy her—a happy wife and mother."

"That's a hit for me. Thank you, Isabel. Am I to understand that you would rather have a husband who had to toil and struggle for every hard-earned penny than possess all the comforts that surround you?" inquired the major, glancing with a complacent air round the well-furnished drawing-room of his country house, in which this conversation took place. "I did not know that your tastes had altered so much, and you cared for the simplicity of poverty!"

"I am in no humour for trifling," exclaimed Isabel, proudly, rising from her seat and passing from the room without bestowing another glance towards her husband.

"I suppose I have offended her highness

at length," said the major to himself, leaning back in his easy-chair. "Heigho, how touchy women are! Upon my honour I do not think I should ever have had the courage to marry if I had known how different they were from the days of courtship. She, evidently would rather have my room than my company down at St. Hilda's, so I think I'll run up to town for a few days, and look up my old friends at the club, and pay my mother a visit."

Accordingly, after putting his wife into the train for St. Hilda's, Major Durant prepared to carry out his resolution, and, arriving in London late in the evening, went to Lady Durant's house.

His visit was as welcome as it was unexpected. His mother expressed no surprise at seeing Lionel without his wife, for their frequent disagreements, which never amounted to serious quarrels, were no secret to her. She knew that her son was not happy with Isabel; that the indifference they had shown to each other before their marriage, now, after four years of wedded life, had increased into something like positive hatred.

Naturally selfish, and fond as ever of his own pleasure, Lionel Durant was perhaps inclined to regard his wife's happiness very lightly; and in return Isabel grew querulous and complaining, when not openly showing her disapproval of nearly all her husband's actions. Both were to blame, for neither showed the slightest forbearance, without which no true content can be found in any relationship of life.

With his mother Lionel found ready sympathy. She had long ceased to expatiate on Isabel's many excellent qualities, which she had formerly held up for his admiration. She was forced to acknowledge that the marriage was a failure, and strove to atone for her eagerness in bringing it to pass by joining in the complaints against Isabel's incompatibility of temper.

Once more amongst the friends of his bachelor days, Major Durant was loth to leave the gaiety of London. His wife wrote to say she was perfectly contented; she had been to the Abbey at Ivor's invitation, and had even met Lord Durant.

"He looks aged and worn; one would take him for quite an old man," the letter said; and the writer knew perfectly well how her husband would resent any approach to friendship with his brother's family; "the working-people at St. Hilda's are loud in their praises of him, and of his goodness and charity; however, he holds himself aloof from all society; his son is obliged to do all the visiting himself: he has grown into a fine, gentlemanly-looking young man, extremely like you in appearance. I am quite anxious to cultivate his acquaintance; he is soon to be married"; and so the letter went on, an apparently friendly, gossiping note, but beneath the surface, discernible only to Lionel's eye, there was hidden a strong desire to show independence, and how little Isabel cared to act according to her husband's desires.

"She is evidently happy where she is, and does not care to return," he explained to his mother; "and I am enjoying myself, so I see no reason to go back to a solitary life. To-night I have arranged with Captain Squills and Harry Fortescue to go to a concert at —— Rooms; and then I have engagements for most evenings during the next fortnight, so I hope Isabel will leave me in peace a little longer."

He took up his hat as he spoke and went out into the street, walking leisurely along with a cigar in his mouth on his way to his club, where he hoped to meet with some of his friends.

In passing a music-shop he turned in to procure a programme for that evening's concert. There were many people being served, and Lionel took a seat, waiting patiently until some one came to attend to his wants.

He was turning over some pieces of music that lay on the counter, in an absent kind of way, and whistling softly below his breath, when presently he became aware of a pair of bright eyes attentively regarding him. A little girl, well dressed, with evident taste, and a desire to show off to the best advantage the exquisite beauty that she possessed, stood near him; a quantity of soft, curling brown hair fell over her shoulders; her hat, which she had just thrown off, lay on the floor beside her, and she was holding out her hands, attracted by the bright-coloured picture on the cover of the song that Major Durant had just taken up.

"Where do you come from, you pretty little creature?" asked the major, stooping down towards her, for he was fond of children.

The child looked up for a moment, half inclined to retreat; its large blue eyes assumed a wild look, and, with an inarticulate cry, she snatched the picture and crumpled it up in her tiny, fat hands, then suddenly seemed inspired with fresh courage, and, approaching, tried to climb on his knee. He raised her in his arms, amused at the confidence and fearlessness with a total stranger, and showed her his watch, smiling at the look of awe and astonishment with which she gazed at the mechanism inside.

"What is your name, little one?" he asked, as she looked up into his face and stole one little plump arm round his neck.

A merry, ringing laugh was the only answer. She was holding the watch to her ear. All at once she started violently, and, dashing the watch aside, uttered a cry of fear or anger, as a servant came up, exclaiming,—

"Fie, for shame, Miss Dolores! that is very rude of you. Come away! You must not be a trouble to the gentleman."

"No, I shan't! go away!" cried the child, struggling and clinging to Lionel as the woman approached to take her from him.

"She is no trouble; let her remain with me; I will take care of her," said Major Durant, for the little girl was fiercely repulsing her attendant.

"What would your ma say, Miss Dolores, you naughty girl!" continued the servant. "She'd give you a good whipping, indeed she would!"

An angry frown on the child's face caused an amused laugh from the major.

"Leave her alone; she is very good with me," he said good-naturedly, and then for a few moments he exerted his ingenuity to keep the child amused, with such success that the rosy face, which fascinated him with its rare beauty, beamed with merry dimpled smiles.

She was standing by his side, looking up with solemn, rapt interest as he talked to her, when her name was called in a voice that caused Lionel to look up with a violent start, and for a second his heart seemed to stand still with the shock.

A lady, closely veiled, and clad in a plain, dark-coloured dress, came forward.

"Dolores my dear, it is time to go home," she said, quietly.

The little girl broke forth into loud passionate sobs, and clung closely to her new friend, and the mother bent down to try and soothe the unaccountably roused burst of grief.

She threw back her veil and looked up; then Major Durant beheld the face that was ever vividly fresh in his mind.

"I am afraid, sir, that my little girl has been troublesome," she began, and then stopped short, and her face turned to a death-like whiteness.

"Mavis!" exclaimed the major.

She did not reply, but with trembling, nerveless fingers she tried to unclasp the little hands that were holding so tightly to Major Durant.

"Oh, Dolores, come away!" she said, in a low voice of entreaty, but the child resolutely refused, kicking and striking at her mother with all the furiously roused anger of a passionate nature. By this time Mavis's face was crimson with emotion and indignation; for a moment her eyes met Lionel's, and then they drooped before his gaze, and catching up the child, heedless of its cries, she put out her hand to command his silence, and then, before the major had recovered from his intense surprise, she had disappeared from his view through an open door at the back of the shop.

He did not wait for her re-appearance. The unexpected meeting had quite unnerved him, and, picking up the broken watch that Dolores had thrown on to the floor in her passion, he turned, and slowly left the shop, continuing his way down the crowded street, walking as if in a dream.

Half an hour afterwards, with a countenance calm and composed, and only the increased pallor of her cheeks proclaiming the emotion she had undergone, Mavis reappeared in the shop, followed by her servant, who carried the still sobbing child, and, taking up the parcel of music that lay ready for her on the counter, she prepared to start home.

The proprietor of the shop came forward and shook hands with her.

"I am afraid my little girl has done mischief, Mr. James," she said, pointing to the torn and crumpled piece of music that lay on the floor.

"Do not apologize, Mrs. Danvers, she does not know any better," was the reply, and Mavis felt that there was a pitying look bent on her as she turned away, and she drew down the veil to hide her starting tears.

"That is Mrs. Danvers, the celebrated singer, who is to appear at —— Rooms to-night, is it not?" asked a lady, as soon as Mavis was out of hearing. "Is that her child?"

"Yes, ma'am," was the reply. "She is much to be pitied, for, as you see, the little girl is likely to prove a great trouble to her; she is not quite right in her head, and I am afraid gets worse."

"Poor creature!—she looks sad, but seems very young and lovely to have such trouble," answered the lady, and then a friend coming up they entered into conversation, and the young singer and her sorrows were forgotten.

"Why, you look as white as a ghost!" was the exclamation of the landlady who opened the door for Mavis on her arrival at her lodgings. "I'm sure you are ill; you haven't been walking, have you?"

"Yes; you know Dolores is always frightened at driving, and she begged so hard to go with me to-day," was the answer.

Mrs. Brown turned impatiently towards the parlour.

"Come, you'd better lie down and rest on the sofa. You've got to sing to-night, and you don't look fit for it, and I'll take the child up to Martha and tell her to keep her quiet, if it is possible, for an hour or so."

"No, no; Dolores must stay with me; Martha cannot manage her; she has not the patience for it: I alone am able to keep her amused."

"Yes, by worrying yourself to death to please her whims! I don't blame the child, she has got no more sense than a new-born babe, although she's going in for four years old. She is sharp enough to get her own way, and after mischief, I can tell you, and if you'll allow me to say it, I think you make her more fractious by humouring her so."

"You do not understand her, Mrs. Brown," exclaimed Mavis, with tears in her eyes. "Perhaps I do indulge my poor little afflicted child; but put yourself in my place, and see if you would not do it. You cannot tell what a trial it is to me. If her mind was only capable of feeling some affection for me I could bear it better. She is all I have to love."

A torrent of hysterical tears drew forth all the kind-hearted woman's sympathy and efforts at consolation. Dolores had thrown herself down on the floor, uttering low, passionate cries; and all her mother's anxious, loving tenderness or the landlady's reproaches would not induce her to look up, or to abate the violent fit of passion that terrified and grieved Mavis.

"My own darling, do try and stop crying," she said at length, bending down, and raising the sobbing child in her arms, gently kissing the tear-stained cheek.

Each cry went to her heart with a sharp pain. It was Lionel after whom Dolores was grieving so sorely, and the thought was one of bitter anguish. "Could he have known who she is?" she asked herself, as she began walking slowly up and down the room.

By-and-by the violence of the child's grief passed away, the sobs grew fainter, and Mavis had the satisfaction of watching the blue-veined lids droop over her eyes, and

Dolores slept, but still a convulsive movement every now and then proclaimed the violence of the emotion that the wild, unchecked nature had undergone.

"You'll make yourself ill carrying about that great heavy child," cried Mrs. Brown, indignantly. "You are so careless about your health. You'll kill yourself if you don't look out; and what will become of her then?—I should like to know. Your face is about the colour of a tallow candle. How long is it since you have had a wink of sleep? I can hear you almost all night moving about your room."

"Not quite so bad as that, Mrs. Brown," said Mavis, with a faint attempt at a smile. "I cannot get much sleep. I generally feel worse at night, and when Dolores is restless I get anxious about her."

"You've more call for anxiety about yourself," was the reply. "Why, I say, what's the matter now?"

Mavis had suddenly stopped. She staggered, and would have fallen had she not caught hold of the table for support.

"Only a sudden giddiness," she said, faintly, moving away to the sofa, and laying the child down.

The cessation of the movement roused Dolores, who began to cry again, and her mother was about to take her up, when Mrs. Brown interposed.

"You shall do no such thing," she said, authoritatively. "You just lie on this sofa until the time comes for you to start to the concert; and, Dolores, look here, your mamma is ill. Come away to Martha, like a good girl, and I'll give you something nice to eat."

But the child was proof against persuasions.

"She does not understand. Let her stay," pleaded Mavis.

However, the landlady was determined, and forcibly took Dolores away; and Mavis, feeling the comfort of silence just then, burdened as she was with painful thoughts, laid her head down to try and obtain some rest. But this was impossible. The distant sound of her child's cries smote on her ear, producing a state of feverish impatience, but which was kept in check by the landlady's stern command of perfect quiet.

At length the passing hours proclaimed the time to prepare for the concert. She rose from the sofa, feeling faint and unrefreshed, after an uneasy slumber of only a few minutes' duration, and going slowly upstairs, she summoned her servant, and commenced her toilet for the evening.

Dolores was reduced to quietness now. She sat perfectly still, watching her mother with interest as she arrayed herself in the pale blue silk that she was to wear that evening, and then Mavis unlocked her dressing-case—one of the only relics of the past days of prosperity that she had retained—and began to turn over in an absent manner the small store of jewellery, as if uncertain what she should wear.

It was an unusual action for one who had ceased to take an interest in her appearance, who never cared to set off the still brilliant beauty which the look of fragile delicacy had increased. At length she opened a small case, and revealed a necklace of pearls resting on deep blue velvet. They were the same that Lord Durant had given her on the day before her wedding.

With a cry of ecstasy Dolores sprang forward,—she had never beheld them before,—and then something prompted Mavis to clasp them round her own fair neck, and watch the little girl's admiration.

"Oh, pretty, pretty!" she cried, clapping her little hands, and, to her mother's surprise, did not seem to wish to possess them, but was perfectly content to admire their beauty.

"Oh, please ma'am, don't take them off," exclaimed the servant, perceiving her mistress about to replace them. "Indeed they look lovely! It would be a real shame."

"Don't take them off," echoed Dolores's lisping accents, and she lifted up her rosy face for a kiss.

Was it a returning touch of vanity, or the unexpected caress on the child's part that caused Mavis to allow the necklace to remain where it was? The tears sprang to her eyes, for the old times had suddenly rushed to her memory; she turned away to hide them from the servant, and with a tender, loving embrace to her child, she took up her gloves and fan and hurried downstairs into the waiting conveyance, and was soon on her way to the concert-room.

CHAPTER X.

DON'T FORGET ME.

Don't forget me, make a shrine to hold me,
  'Tis one treasure from all else apart ;
Weave a web of happy thoughts to fold me,
  Safe in life and death, within your heart.
H. M. BURNSIDE.

"What's the matter with you, Durant, old fellow? You look as sad as if you'd lost a fortune. Come, cheer up! I dare say you'll have something worth hearing to-night, if you are fond of music." So said Captain Squills, one of Major Durant's friends, as they drove together towards —— Rooms.

The unusual silence and thoughtfulness that had fallen on Lionel Durant had afforded much amusement and wonder to his friends, who were wont to see him gay and light-hearted. He heeded not their joking comments, for the meeting with Mavis had affected him so deeply, that he could not easily shake off the recollection of her sweet pale face. It was some comfort to him when the commencement of the concert brought the cessation of their remarks; he could fold his arms, lean back in his seat, and give himself over to undisturbed thoughts.

What did it matter to him that the music was sounding near him, ravishingly sweet, enchaining a large audience in breathless attention? It fell on an ear deadened to the beauty of the perfectly rendered symphony or sonata; his heart was far away; and his eyes, wandering from the instrumentalists, were apparently intently studying the programme he held in his hands. His two friends were listening or enthusiastically applauding, too busy to notice his preoccupation.

At length there came a pause; Lionel did not notice it, but mechanically followed the example of others, and turned to the next song, without looking up.

It commenced. A few chords of prelude, and then, exquisitely soft and sweet, the first purely clear notes fell on his ear. He looked up then, his heart beating, his face flushed. *She* who was present in his thoughts stood before him, and it was her voice that appealed to his senses in the words she sang :—

> " Don't forget me, make a shrine to hold me
>   Safe and warm within your faithful heart;
> Weave a web of happy thoughts to fold me
>   In all dear remembrance when we part.
>
> " If some song I have been wont to sing you,
>   Or the perfume of some flower or tree
> Steals across your senses, let it bring you
>   Silent messages of love from me."

Major Durant was interested at last. There was a hush in the room, followed by a subdued murmur, when the verse came to an end. He heeded it not, each note was stealing into his heart; it seemed as if she sang alone for him. The pale face, the fragile, almost dazzling beauty, nearly overcame him. He could scarcely realize that it was not all a dream. He could not withdraw his gaze from her face, though the very sight was painful to him. And then, slowly, the mournful eyes sought the page of music, and she went on:—

> "Don't forget me if the world should grieve you,
>   If your life's fair hopes should fail or fade;
> Summer friends and summer lovers leave you,
>   Don't forget, I love you in the shade."

Were the words addressed to him? She was looking his way. The walls of the room seemed closing round him; he was conscious of only one presence. Presently a start, as with an electric shock, a look of recognition, and the glance of the singer met that fixed on her face. It was only momentary; in another second she had recovered her self-possession. The music seemed invested with a new beauty—a plaintive, appealing ring of sadness:—

> "A weary while of absence must betide us,
>   Before I see your face or clasp your hand;
> But even if death's shadow should divide us,
>   Love lives on in the eternal land.

> "Don't forget me——"

A pause. The notes ended in a smothered cry. A heavy fall, and the fair singer lay motionless.

There was a sudden rush to the spot where she had fallen; musicians, singers, and audience all pressed forward; and Lionel Durant found himself forcing his way, with maddened anxiety, through the throng that opposed his passage. He reached her side; he bent over the silent form in speechless dread; her blue eyes, that had so often beamed on him with tenderness and love, were closed now, and the fair cheek was as pale as death.

He would have given worlds to have pressed a kiss on those pallid, unconscious lips, but he was there as a stranger. There were voices authoritatively commanding him to stand back, which recalled his scattered faculties.

They raised her up, and she was borne from his sight. The pearls had fallen from her neck: they lay unnoticed on the floor. Without a second's pause for reflection, he had possessed himself of them, and slipped them into his pocket.

"A sudden faintness," he heard some one say. "She was overcome with the heat of the room. There was a medical man amongst the audience; he is with her, and she is reviving now."

These tidings sent a ray of comfort into Lionel's soul. His two friends had come up, and he felt himself forced to reply to their questions and expressions of surprise at the occurrence that had proved an interruption to the harmony of the evening.

Presently some order was restored in the audience. The director of the concert came forward with a speech apologizing for the unavoidable delay in the performance, and repeating the surgeon's declaration that the seizure, though dangerous, was now passing off, and the concert would presently recommence, and the remainder of the programme would be carried out, with the exception of the songs allotted to Mrs. Danvers.

Major Durant was restless and impatient; he could not even make a pretence of listening to the music that followed; his mind was occupied with thoughts of Mavis. Twice in that one day he had seen her, and each glimpse of the beautiful face, on which such unmistakable suffering was written, had filled him with horror. Was it his doing? Had he caused the visible change, the transparent whiteness, the hectic flush, that revealed so plainly the gradual decay?

She had recognized him; he had noticed the look of agonized reproach that had flitted across her features as their eyes met, and he felt that never to his dying day could he get rid of the recollection of that one sorrowful glance. He never knew how he contrived to assume an appearance of partial composure during the remainder of the evening at the club, to which his friends insisted on his accompanying them. He was only conscious of an amazing sense of rest and comfort when he found himself once more alone in the quiet of his mother's house. He drew forth the pearl necklace, and then for the first time the knowledge of the risk he had run in taking possession of it flashed into his mind with an uncomfortable sensation. He had not given one thought to its value, and that it would be missed and a search instituted as soon as Mavis became aware of the loss she had sustained.

"I suppose I should be regarded as a thief," he said to himself, and the idea would have caused him to laugh outright had not graver, sadder thoughts occupied his mind. "I must find some means of restoring it. Perhaps it may lead to an interview." The bare prospect brought a thrill of gladness and hope which he did not care to struggle against, and all through the night he was thinking of that silent, motionless form, that had recalled to him the memory of the only love that had ever dwelt in his heart.

The sudden illness of the young singer had excited much sympathy, and many were the kind messages sent from those who were present at the concert. The heat of the room was the cause assigned by the surgeon who attended her, and, in answer to the questions put to him, he predicted that, after rest and quiet for a few days, she would be able to resume her professional duties. But when alone with Mrs. Brown, who waited on

Mavis with unremitting care and attention, he looked grave; the attack was more serious than he cared to reveal to every one. He saw that Mavis suspected it; her sad look, and the mournful tenderness with which she was evidently thinking of her child's future, convinced him that she perceived how slowly but surely she was fading away.

"My mother died of a sort of decline," she said, one morning, three days after the concert; "and I have led a troubled life. I feel as if I shall never get much better." In vain the surgeon tried to reassure her; she only shook her head. "You are trying to deceive me," she continued. "Do you think I can have gone on all this time, getting weaker and weaker, and not have known how it must end?" Her eyes filled with tears as they wandered towards Dolores, who was playing near her mother's sofa, and the surgeon perceived the significance of that sad glance. With a few cheering words, but without a further attempt to deny that which was so clearly revealed to Mavis's mind, he took his leave, after a parting injunction to his patient to keep quiet and unexcited.

But quietness and peace were not destined to be Mavis's lot any more in life. Soon Dolores wearied of her game, came to claim the attention of her mother, who readily gave up the rest she so much needed to devote herself to her child's amusement. She raised herself slowly from the sofa, and, opening the piano, began to play and sing in a low sweet voice some simple melodies that caused the little girl (over whose restless mind music possessed almost the only influence) to cease her wailing cry, and stand quietly listening to the sounds.

But Mavis's heart was sad, whilst her fingers moved swiftly over the keys, producing merry sounds that jarred discordantly with her present frame of mind. The silent tears were rolling down her pale cheeks, whilst Dolores, laughing happily, was dancing about the room in childish glee.

Presently the door was thrown open.

"A gentleman to see you, ma'am," said the servant, showing in a visitor.

Mavis rose from the music-stool, turned round, and found herself face to face with Major Durant!

It almost seemed as if her eyes had deceived her—that it could not be Lionel who stood before her. It must be a dream! but, no; he advanced, holding out his hand, and with the old cordial smile that she remembered far too well.

With an effort Mavis subdued the wild fluttering of her heart. She could not clasp his proffered hand; she merely bowed and silently motioned him to a seat.

"I have come as a friend, Mavis. How could I stay away when I knew you were weak and suffering?" he began, but his voice trembled as he spoke. "Can you forgive me?"

She had remained standing all the time. She felt his earnest, searching gaze fixed on her face, and she knew that he perceived the ravages that grief and illness had wrought; and now she shrank back, and, in spite of all her efforts at calmness, she burst into tears.

"Why did you come? Could you not have left me alone? It will not be much longer that I have to endure this terribly hard existence."

She sobbed, covering her face as if to hide out the sight of him.

Major Durant did not reply. He allowed her to exhaust her passionate grief. He had scarcely realized what the meeting would be, but had simply followed the impulse that prompted him once more to see and speak with Mavis, and to restore the necklace to its owner.

"You are ill!" he exclaimed, at length. "Oh, Mavis! how can I forgive myself?—for I feel that I have caused all this!"

"It is too late to think of that now, Major Durant!" answered Mavis, forcing back her tears, and trying to look steadily into the gloomy face before her. "My heart is broken. I shall soon find rest: but, oh, my child, poor little darling, whose life I have blighted so terribly!"

During this conversation Dolores had approached timidly to the major's side. He took her up on his knee, and bent his face over her to hide his emotion.

"It cannot be so!" he cried, impulsively. "Mavis, you must try and live; you may yet be happy!"

"Never, never!" she answered. "Happiness is not for me! You are only seeking to deceive me. Is it not a vain wish? Could you really desire this miserable life to continue? No! it is useless to conceal the truth; I have known for a long time that I am dying; and can you wish it otherwise?"

Major Durant sprang from his seat and set Dolores down.

"Mavis, do not talk like that!" he cried. "My love! why do you utter the words that are torturing me with reproach?" He had come up close to her, and taken both her hands. "Look up, my darling: for I cannot bear this!"

"Then why did you come here? You must have foreseen that this would be our last interview—that the time has come for us to say, 'Good-bye.' Oh, how can I bring myself to speak those words!"

Her sentence ended in a sobbing cry of anguish; but it revealed to him that cruelly as it had been tried, the love for him still dwelt in her memory.

"Is there nothing I can do? Am I powerless to give you comfort, Mavis? I too have suffered keenly from the thoughts of my conduct to you; but I was driven to it,—I had to choose between my mother's love and yours."

"And naturally you chose the former. Perhaps you were right, Lionel. Our paths in life lay in opposite directions: you acted so as to deserve the credit of the world, whilst I—well, never mind about that; it is weak and foolish to be for ever dwelling on the dark side of life."

She looked up with a vain attempt at a smile, but her lips were quivering.

"Do you not think it would be better to part now?" she asked, facing him bravely.

"Perhaps so," he replied. "But are there not other subjects about which you wish to speak? You mentioned fears for your child's future. Will you trust her to me? I have the best right when—when—"

He hesitated, but Mavis continued,—

"When I am dead. Oh, Lionel, if she could only go with me! How can she be capable of fighting her way through all the hard troubles of life? You must have perceived that she is not like other children."

"Yes, I have noticed it; but is that not an additional reason that I should pity her, and try and make her life smooth? Cannot you trust me? Ah, you little know what I would give for a child to inherit my name; there are no little ones to gladden my home. Mavis, I am a wretched man! I, too, have suffered keenly; and when the longings come for that which might have been—for the happiness I carelessly thrust aside—it nearly drives me to desperation."

"It seems all a bitter mistake, but I must be the one to bear the degradation unto the end. No, Lionel, I will bind you to no promises; your duty is with your wife—to consider her wishes," said Mavis, in a low voice.

"Then it must be so," replied the major, sadly, in a tone that revealed, more than words, the misery that he felt. "One brief glimpse of sunshine, and now I must go back to my desolate life, unloved and unloving—it is a just requital."

"The last time!" whispered Mavis. "You will not see me again." Her face was half averted; it seemed to have taken a fresh radiance of beauty, in the melancholy smile that illumined the now calm, lovely features.

His arm was round her waist; he drew her towards him, and his lips were pressed to hers.

"There is surely no harm in it," he said, as he wrung her hand in silence. "If ever you need anything, Mavis, do not scruple to send to me. You once refused my help; will you do so now?"

"I do not want for anything," she replied, steadily. "For myself I never shall; should others need it, I will write my requests. Now, please go. Why should you prolong this misery?"

He walked to the door, and then, hesitating, turned back.

"Can you pardon my presumption, Mavis? I saw this lying on the floor where you had fallen," he said, producing the pearl necklace from his pocket. "Without thinking, with only a desire to possess something that belonged to you, I retained it. My object in coming to-day was to restore it to you."

He still kept it in his hand, apparently not perceiving that she had put out hers to take it from him. Suddenly he looked up.

"I cannot give it back," he cried, quickly. "You have worn it: I saw it on your neck when you fell fainting, when your eyes revealed that which was a bitter sting to my faithlessness. May I keep it as a memento of you, my only loved one?"

"No, Major Durant!" Mavis cried vehemently, "I shall not give it to you. To me it speaks of better, purer love than yours ever was. Those pearls were given to me by your brother!"

As Mavis uttered these words, she threw herself down on to the sofa, weeping passionate, bitter tears, keeping her face resolutely turned from him.

Slowly and reluctantly he laid the necklace on the table, and with one sorrowful look towards Mavis he was gone from the house.

He was gone, and she should never see him again. This was the one thought that was above all others in Mavis's heart. All was forgotten in her bitter trouble. His cruel desertion of her was forgiven now; she could not feel anything but sympathy for the man she had loved once and for always. "Poor Lionel! I can see he is unhappy, and I can afford to pity him now," she said; and the thought that perhaps he needed her pity made her heart relent towards him. "Who knows how he may have been tried! and all this time I have allowed angry feelings to remain in my heart. He must think me cruel and unforgiving for having spoken coldly; but, oh, if he only knew how I was striving to hide my real feelings! I wonder if I have acted rightly in refusing help for Dolores; if my pride has caused me to forget my darling's welfare? Oh, that I had some friend to advise or tell me what to do!"

And then her thoughts wandered back through the past years. She thought of Lord Durant, and of his true, faithful love, that now, when too late, she knew was so far beyond what she deserved. Did he ever think of her? she wondered; or had the lapse of time taught him to regard her conduct harshly. "Some day he will hear of me when I am dead; perhaps in his heart he may have some kind thoughts for one who made him suffer the misery which I myself have since undergone."

The kind-hearted landlady began to wonder what had caused the unusual look of sadness in her lodger's face, after the interview with the major. And when, in her childish conversation, Dolores alluded to the "kind gentleman who had been to see her," she noticed how the tears dimmed the now-fading blue eyes, and that an expression of anguish crossed her pale face.

Day by day Mavis grew weaker and

thinner; to those constantly about her the change was not visible, it was so gradual. Each week some little duty had to be given up. At first it was only the daily walk with Dolores, and then by degrees the number of pupils had to be diminished; even in her own home, Mavis found it impossible to continue her teaching; and then, to add to her troubles, once more the cold shadow of poverty approached nearer.

Then her child fell ill of some infantile complaint, and there was an additional expense of medical attendance to be incurred, as well as the anxiety that robbed the mother of the rest that she needed so sorely, for all the time she could spare had to be devoted to the care of her fretful, suffering child.

All her ornaments had to be sold—even the pearl necklace; the sight of it, the recollections and mingled emotions it called up when she brought it forth, caused her to shed many bitter tears. She would fain have kept it. To have it sent to Lionel, after her death, had been her wish—there could have been no harm in letting him have some token of forgiveness when she was laid in the grave, she thought; but her child's wants were the first consideration, so the pearls were obliged to go.

The money they fetched was already due in payment of bills that had been contracted. The London season was over; there was little chance of obtaining concert engagements, especially after a long illness that had robbed the once-beautiful voice of much of its strength and purity.

And, as if to add to her troubles, there came another parting that had to be endured. Mavis was obliged to quit the home that had been hers for so many years. She had grown quite attached to the place and to the landlady, from whom she had received so much kindness, but the house had to be given up.

One of Mrs. Brown's sons, who had settled in Australia, wrote to offer his mother a home with him.

It was not until she had gone that Mavis began to realize how true a friend this woman had been to her; and now she was once more alone in the world, ill and suffering, not knowing where to turn for a kind word of sympathy.

"Will this all end in having to apply to Lionel for help?" Mavis asked herself, as she sat before the small fire, on the chilly, damp autumn day on which she and Dolores first took up their abode in the cheap, dingy lodgings to which necessity compelled them to go. It was a dreary look-out into a narrow street, inhabited by a low, toiling population, amongst whom the little singer felt doubly lonely; but she could not afford to be particular. "One more struggle, and I shall be compelled to lay aside the pride that keeps me from telling him of my wants. If it were only for myself, I could endure this; but oh, Dolores, it breaks my heart to see you unhappy!"

At the sound of her name the child came forward, and, in her broken, lisping accents, began a lament about the discomfort she found round her, and the untempting food that was all her mother could afford to purchase now.

Mavis looked anxiously into the little tear-stained face; it was very pale and thin. The surgeon was right when he had said that Dolores needed strengthening food, such as lay beyond her power to give.

"If I could only get some employment!" she cried, in despair. "Anything, however hard, would be better than this."

Each wailing cry from her child went to her heart, and she was powerless to soothe the distress; but how could Dolores understand? Her mind was not capable of realizing how she was adding to her mother's illness by her constant complaint. As she passed up and down the narrow staircase that led to her room, Mavis noticed occasional glances of pity from the rough-looking women who inhabited the other rooms in the house.

"That poor lady upstairs ain't far off her grave," she heard one woman say. "She gets thinner and paler every week. She's almost worn to a shadow now: poor thing! she seems to have no friends."

Loud and coarse as the tones were, Mavis could not resist looking up gratefully at the speaker; for a single word of kindly sympathy was precious now,—it cheered her up a little, and took away some of the dreadful despondency that ill health and poverty had brought.

"Just one more trial, my darling, before I write to Major Durant," she said, stooping down to kiss her child, before she set out to battle with the wind and rain of a cold November afternoon, that was so trying to her enfeebled strength, in her weary search for employment: what it was she did not care, if she could only earn money to provide comforts for Dolores. "One more struggle; and, if it is successful, pride must be cast aside. Stay quietly here, my child, until mother comes back to you."

"Take me with you!" pleaded Dolores.

But Mavis was obliged to refuse. The cold was too great for the delicate child; besides, she herself felt too weak and ill to undertake the care of the restless little girl along the narrow crowded streets through which she had to pass.

"Do not cry like that! I will try and

come back soon!" she said, almost irritably. It was the first time she had ever spoken angrily to Dolores, and her heart smote her reproachfully, as she went downstairs, and the child's appealing, passionate cries reached her ear.

It was a sound that dwelt long in her mind, and as she slowly pursued her way up the street the cry seemed to haunt her, and she hurried on to the utmost of her power, in her anxiety to again rejoin her child.

CHAPTER XI.

A FRIEND IN NEED.

The mouth with steady sweetness set,
  The eyes conveying, unaware,
The distant hint of some regret
  That harboured there.
                              J. INGELOW.

"HALLO! look out there! Do you want to be run over?"

These words, uttered in gruff tones, startled Mavis, and caused her to turn round suddenly. She had wandered on aimlessly, her mind filled with her own sad thoughts. It was all the same to her which way she went; she was trusting to a vague chance that something might turn up in this dismal wilderness of misery.

Half blinded with the thick folds of her

veil and the tears that filled her eyes, she did not perceive that she had reached a narrow thoroughfare, and was recklessly passing through the crowd of vehicles, until the above words recalled her to the danger of her position.

She stood irresolute, uncertain whether to advance or to retreat. A heavily laden van blocked the road, and in the other direction a hansom cab dashed rapidly towards her. The driver pulled up his horse, but it was too late. In another moment she would have been struck down, had not a strong arm drawn her back; and then she felt herself swiftly piloted through the crowd, until she reached the opposite footpath.

Mavis looked up to thank her preserver. He was a tall, rather powerful-looking young man, not without a certain claim to good looks; but there was an air of vulgarity in his threadbare shabby clothes and the conspicuous display of gilt watch-chain, an several imitation rings adorned his not over clean hands.

But with all this there was something in

his appearance that was familiar to Mavis. She looked again, wondering where she had seen him before, when, with a loud laugh, he cried out,—

"Why, Mavis! who would have expected to see you?" and seizing her unwilling hand he gave it a hearty shake. "Is that all the welcome you can give to your cousin?"

"Are you really my cousin, Edward Austin?" she asked, wonderingly, as the fact of who it really was flashed into her mind.

"Yes, himself, and no other; but I say, Mavis, you aren't ashamed of me, are you? because I'm not one to intrude myself," was the answer, given in lower, gentler tones. "You are not looking as if life was easy with you just now. I should scarcely have known you, you look so ill, but handsomer than ever."

Even coming from such a man as Edward Austin evidently was, the sound of a friendly voice gave inexpressible comfort to Mavis's desolate heart. She noticed how the rough, bold manner softened to respect, as he accommodated his pace to hers, and kept by her side.

"Here! don't take that turning," he said, as they approached one of the better class of streets. "You will not like to be seen walking with such a fellow as I am, by the swell people you know; but I want to hear something about you: shall we keep straight on?"

"It is all the same to me where I go," quietly answered Mavis. "I have no friends in London; I am alone."

"Ah, yes, I have heard," said Edward. "As soon as I got out of gaol (I was in for three years, you know) I went to St. Hilda's. I thought I'd find you there, and perhaps you'd help me on a little; and when I was there I heard what had happened, and found my old enemy, Ivor Morgan, established at the Abbey. There are some strange ups and downs in the world; and to think that you weren't Lady Durant after all!"

"Don't talk of it please, Edward, I cannot bear it just yet," pleaded Mavis, in a choked voice. "I have been very, very miserable."

"To be sure you have! I should like to give that scoundrel, Major Durant, a good horsewhipping for his conduct," savagely exclaimed the young man, with a fierce oath. "What right had he to behave as he did to such a pretty little creature as you are!"

Mavis's tears were falling fast; these words brought all her misery before her mind.

"Please not to say such things!" she asked, as soon as she could find words to speak. "I would rather not be reminded of all I have suffered; I wish you would talk of something else."

There was forced composure in her voice, and she tried to speak carelessly, but Edward possessed sufficient discernment to read much in the expressive face.

"I have not thanked you yet," she went on to say, "for your kindness a few minutes ago. I had no idea I was in danger until I heard your warning."

"Didn't you hear the people shouting to you? I expected to see you under the wheels every second. It was a lucky escape; but I had no idea at the time that it was my cousin whose life I saved."

"It was very good of you," answered Mavis, shuddering, when she thought of her narrow escape. "It was my carelessness that led me into danger; I was thinking of other things, and not looking where I was going."

"Why, what's the matter? How pale you have gone! Are you ill?" interrupted the young man, suddenly arresting his pace.

"It's only a little faintness. It will soon pass off," answered Mavis, pressing her hand to her side. "Don't look so frightened: I shall be all right directly."

"But I say!" continued her cousin. "You are not fit to be up and about. You ought to be safe at home, and have a surgeon to attend you: wait a second, I will bring you something to set you up."

He was gone in a moment; and Mavis closed her eyes, and leant back against the wall by which she was standing. The roar of the street traffic sounded far distant; all seemed to be fading away from her senses.

Presently Edward Austin returned, with a glass of brandy in his hand; he forced Mavis to drink some of it, and it revived her.

"And now give me your address," he said. "I shall call a cab to take you home."

"Oh, no, no, I can manage to walk very well now," exclaimed Mavis, in remonstrance. "I would far rather do so."

"It's a likely thing that I shall allow it; come—don't be foolish!" he began, moving away to hail a passing cab.

"But I'm not going home," persisted Mavis. "I have business to do. I came out in search of employment, and I cannot go back again until I get some; for I am very poor."

"And what is Major Durant thinking about to allow it?" asked Edward, indignantly, but Mavis interrupted him.

"It is my own choice," she said. "He must not be blamed; he offered to help me.

But I have been ill. I owe money to pay the doctor's bill, and I cannot obtain concert engagements."

"You keep up your singing then?" asked Edward eagerly.

"Yes," she answered, "but of course my chances of getting on are gone now, and I have no influence to obtain engagements."

"You say you are poor; are you particular what you do so that you can earn something?" was the next question.

"I have no right to be particular for my child's sake," faltered Mavis.

By this time the cab that Edward Austin hailed had drawn up close by the pavement where they stood.

"If you'll get in here," he continued, "I'll come and see you to-morrow. Mind, I give you no promises, but I'll see what I can do for you."

Mavis knew that further resistance was useless; she suffered her cousin to place her in the vehicle.

"Where shall I tell him to drive to?" he asked, as he closed the door.

Mavis gave the required address.

"Good-bye, keep up your spirits," he said, cheerfully, putting his head in at the window as the horse slowly moved away. "I've settled with the driver."

He raised his hat to her, and turned away without giving her time to express her thanks.

The unexpected kindness, coming as it did just in time to save her from utter despair, cheered Mavis's drooping spirits. She noticed genuine pity beneath her cousin's rough, rather vulgar manner; he had spoken of future employment, and, whatever it was, she felt strong hope rising, where only before had been gloomy despondency. It was with a lighter heart than she had felt for a long time that she ascended the steep uncarpeted stairs that led to her room. When she reached the landing she stopped to rest, for the ascent always tried her now. The door of her room stood open, and as she listened she heard the sound of a strange voice, and caught sight of a tall dark figure standing there, in conversation with Dolores.

With a feeling of surprise, for visitors seldom came to see her, Mavis hurried forward.

The stranger turned her head, and Mavis perceived a face not altogether unfamiliar to her. Her dress was studiously plain, and marked her out as a member of some charitable sisterhood. Mavis had several times seen ladies similarly attired going about in the neighbourhood in which she now lived, and often in cases of sickness or necessity they had visited some of the lodgers in that very house. Therefore her first surprise quickly vanished, and she advanced into the room.

In an instant Dolores had come up to her mother's side, and in her imperfect language was beginning an almost unintelligible story, when the stranger interposed.

"I found your little girl out in the street; she had lost her way, and was in great distress, so I have taken the liberty of bringing her home, as I was passing at the time."

"Thank you, thank you; I am very much obliged to you," exclaimed Mavis, clasping her child in her arms, for Dolores had begun to sob passionately at the sight of her mother.

She felt the stranger's eyes fixed on her with a look of interest; she threw back her veil and glanced up, as she uttered her heartfelt thanks, and then for the first time their eyes met. With a cry of horror Mavis sprang back, and covered her pale face, whilst all the sadness of her life, all her bitter sorrow, rushed on her in a moment.

"Oh, why did you come to me! Did *he* send you to see how wretched I am? Do not come near me: I am not fit even to speak to you."

"Then you know me?" asked Sister Veronica (for the new-comer was she), in a calm voice, in which no emotion could be discerned. "And, if I judge aright by your looks, it is not altogether chance that brings me here. You are unhappy: am I not the fittest person to help you?"

"Do not you hate me, who was so long your unconscious supplanter?" asked Mavis, speaking with difficulty through her sobs.

"Hate you! no. Why should I do so, when you seem to need pity and comfort? Yours has been a wicked, misspent life; but I see it is useless to reproach you. It is too late now; your face tells me that your days are already numbered."

"Don't blame me; it is your pity that I need!" sobbed Mavis. "You say that I am dying. I know it. And what is to become of this child—my poor, forsaken little Dolores, whose future comfort, and perhaps happiness, I have overthrown through my wicked pride?"

Completely overcome with fatigue, illness, and the revulsion of feeling through which she had passed, Mavis's tears fell faster; and then the cold manner that was almost habitual to Sister Veronica, and was only overcome by strong emotion, such as had induced her to seek out Mavis, began to thaw a little, and her next words were uttered in a kinder, gentler tone. The deeper feelings of her heart had been roused; the sympathy that she instinctively felt for those to whom she could give help was called forth, and, before long, she had drawn from Mavis some account of her sufferings and privations.

At last, when the first paroxysm of distress was over, Mavis was persuaded by her visitor to lie down. It was an unspeakable relief to be able to lay her throbbing brow on the soft pillow, to be aware of the sudden cessation of Dolores' voice, and to feel the consciousness of a kind, gentle presence soothing her pain and weariness. Two or three times she re-opened her heavy eyes to convince herself that it was not all a dream, but a reality.

"I thought you were still in Rome: I did not know you had come back to England," she said, after a long silence, during which she had watched the tall, darkly clad figure moving noiselessly about, preparing food for Dolores, who for once sat happy and contented by the table.

"I have been some weeks in London," was the answer. "It was my son who first suggested that a field of usefulness lay before me in this great city. He begged me to come and be near him."

"Yes; I remember. Ivor is your son," said Mavis, dreamily. "How strange it all seems—that dark time that made a wreck of my life! Does he live at St. Hilda's? Oh, do tell me something," she went on, in imploring accents. "I want to know about—those who were so kind to me—so much better than I deserved." Mavis hesitated, for she could not bear to utter Lord Durant's name.

Sister Veronica forcibly suppressed the slight shade of emotion that crossed her features.

"Lord Durant still lives on at the Abbey," she answered, averting her face. "His life is given up to deeds of goodness. I suppose he is happy; he ought to be so."

She was hard and cold, so Mavis thought, and a momentary feeling of dislike entered her mind: but then the cool hand was laid on her heated, feverish forehead, and the pain seemed to disappear, as if by magic, beneath that light touch.

"You are very kind—much too good for such an one as I am," said Mavis, looking up gratefully. "Will you come and see me again some day? Is it asking too much?—I have no friends left in the world."

And after promising to pay another visit Sister Veronica took her departure along the narrow, dismal streets, until she came to her own small, plain lodging, where she had come, on first resolving to devote herself to her self-imposed duty.

In quitting the convent she had not laid aside the dress or the strict rules of the order to which she had adhered, though bound by no vows, but had resolved to live independently, thus being enabled to go about alone and unquestioned in her efforts to seek out and help Mavis. She now kept up a constant correspondence with Ivor. The affection for her son, which dated from the time they had spent together during Claude Monticth's illness, was the only link that bound her to the outer world. In all other respects the whole of her life was absorbed in similar self-denying tasks to those that she had devoted herself to so many years before.

And when she reached her homely little parlour a letter that had come during her absence lay on the table. It was from Ivor—a long letter covering many sheets. It was to tell of his marriage with Jessie, which had taken place a few days before; and in her mind's eye Sister Veronica could picture quite clearly the quiet country church on the hill-side at Pen Vychan, where the sound of the waves could be heard, and the white-robed bride, whose features were rendered familiar by Ivor's description: the tall, fine-looking bridegroom, and the white-haired, saddened figure standing beneath the shadows of the old edifice, the broad, intellectual brow, lined with care and sadness,—the solemn words that the clergyman had uttered,—all this rushed through Sister Veronica's brain. It seemed like a vision; it was as if the dingy, smoke-begrimed room in which she sat had suddenly grown larger. She heard the words from the marriage-service echoing in her brain. Twice in her life she had heard the service of the English Church—only twice, and yet the words, "till death us do part," were returning into her mind. She bent her head, and for once the cold grey eyes were filled with tears of bitter repentance.

It had never come home to her before, until she held in her hand the letter containing the news of her son's wedding, how much to blame her past conduct was, her want of forbearance, her desertion of her husband in his time of need.

"He needed me more than ever then!" she said to herself, amid her sobs. "My cruelty robbed me of my son, and I thought to atone for my sin by works of piety; but never, ah, never can I know true comfort and rest."

Then her thoughts reverted to the pallid face that she had seen that afternoon,—the dying little creature whom she had despised, even while showing kindness to her, feeling herself superior to the wretched woman whose words of gratitude were still ringing in her ears.

"But am I really much better than she is?" she asked herself—"I who have thought myself above most of my fellow-creatures, without ever reverting to my past actions."

The unexpected meeting with Mavis, to accomplish which she had spent much time in fruitless search and inquiry, had made a deep impression on her mind. The brief interview in the artist's room at Rome had been long enough to reveal to her the excessive beauty of the woman whom Lord Durant had loved so truly, but now, beholding her again with the patient suffering that cast a halo of extra loveliness on the delicate features, had driven all other feelings, but those of pity, from her mind.

"And this must be my resolve," she said to herself. "For Lord Durant's sake I must watch over her; I must not let her die in want; and when it is all over I must find means to let him know that the misery is ended, for his love must have been strong to have survived through all."

True to his promise the next morning Edward Austin presented himself at his cousin's lodgings. He came in rather noisily, with a hearty greeting, expressed his commiseration at the sight of Mavis's pale looks, and then began to unfold the object of his visit.

"I have good news for you," he said, rubbing his hands together, as he drew forward a chair and sat down.

"Something for me to do; that is very kind of you," said Mavis, wearily, for she felt too dispirited to brighten up even at the prospect of earning money for Dolores.

"I can't just come to terms about the salary," continued the young man; "I spoke to my friend Bennett, the manager of the X. Theatre. He is a 'cute one: he says he'll see how you get on first. I told him you were first rate—something different from what's ever heard on his boards; but he'd rather wait a bit."

"Is it at a theatre?" asked Mavis; "I was in hopes of getting a concert engagement. I do not much like the idea of acting: besides you should not have spoken so highly of my attainments; I am not sure if I could act at all."

"Oh, it's mostly singing that you'll have

to do," was the careless reply. "They are getting up a comic Christmas piece; it will be rare fun, and will serve to raise your spirits a little: so cheer up; you frighten a fellow when you look so downcast, for I have made an appointment for you to see the manager this very day, and here I am to go and introduce you, so now it's too late to draw back."

"I have not the slightest intention of disappointing your friend," answered Mavis, quietly. "As I told you before, I cannot afford to be particular. I am ready to go with you any time."

"All right. The sooner the better. Put on your bonnet. It isn't far to go. Only I wish you were not quite so pale and delicate looking. I'm afraid Bennett may not like it."

"I cannot help it. I am stronger than I look," answered Mavis, with a sad attempt at a smile, as she prepared to set out with her cousin.

The errand was successful. Mavis obtained the appointment; and although the salary was very small—much too small for the arduous duties required of her—she thankfully accepted it, in hopes that it might lead to something better in time.

Before crowded audiences Mavis had to appear night after night. She had to disguise the weary, aching sadness, and to listen, with a smile which seemed a mockery to her misery, to the plaudits of those for whose pleasure, and to earn a miserable pittance, she was bound to appear, in spite of the increasing weakness that made it a toil to raise her pure, sweet voice, and sing the words that produced peals of laughter, but found no echo of response in her heart; for how could she feel happy, although she had to strive to throw off the oppression that was slowly robbing her of life?

It was a hitherto unknown degradation, and often when she was singing the sweet melodies that were delighting the ears of the audience the unshed tears were smarting beneath her eyelids, whilst a smile that to a close observer had a painful pathos in it was to be seen on her lips.

Sister Veronica often came to see her during that long, dreary winter, and into her ears Mavis poured the tale of her present sorrows.

But, although she sympathized with the singer's unhappiness, she made no effort to deliver her from the life that was so inexpressibly painful. Sister Veronica deemed that the trial would prove salutary; for how could she tell that Mavis had long ago learned the lesson of humility, and that this further degradation was only hastening the end, against which she now no longer made an attempt to struggle?

CHAPTER XII.

ONCE AGAIN.

Oh, would it were my lot
To be forgetful as I am forgot!
BYRON.

THE dreary, dismal winter, with its ceaseless round of degrading work, of heart-rending despair, was over, and the bright spring sunshine brought a faint ray of hope into Mavis's aching heart. She still struggled against her increasing weakness, living solely for her child's sake, and each evening appeared before the audience in the small dingy theatre, where she still found means of earning the little that sufficed for the bare necessaries of life for herself and Dolores. How she had lived through the winter nobody but herself knew. She rarely spoke of herself to those with whom her occupation brought her in contact, and there were few who cared to inquire about the sleepless nights of pain and weariness, of days passed in feverish endeavours to bear up and preserve her strength for the evening's ordeal.

"It is a wonder she has lived so long," were the words that were uttered often within her hearing, until at last Mavis began to wonder herself. She dare not look back over the fearful time of hardship and privation, the sting of which was rendered doubly hard to bear by the weakness that craved for rest.

But the bright, warm sunbeams, streaming in through the window of her room, seemed to bring with them a new spring of life, and in the season when all nature was putting on a fresh radiance of verdure, the pale, wan cheeks assumed a hectic flush that seemed to promise a return of health. It was merely a delusive hope. However, it served to raise Mavis's drooping spirits.

"Perhaps I shall get well after all," she said to Dolores one afternoon, when she lay on the faded, chintz-covered sofa, and felt the gentle spring breeze fanning her heated forehead.

It was almost as if in answer to her last words that a well-known heavy footstep was heard ascending the stairs, and, after a preliminary knock, Edward Austin came in. He had evidently prepared for the visit, for, instead of his ordinary rough clothes, he wore a neat dark suit, with less conspicuous display of watch-chain than usual, and in his button-hole he carried a small bunch of flowers.

"Are you going out for a holiday?" asked Mavis, with a faint smile, as soon as she had cordially greeted him, for she had learned to look forward to his visits with pleasure. Rough and uncouth as he was, in her forlorn desolation she could fully appreciate his good-natured kindness to her.

"Yes, I have an afternoon to myself," he answered; "and so I have come to take you and Dolores out for a bit of a stroll.

Will you go with me? It will do you good. We can go by omnibus all the way, so it won't tire you; and then we can sit and watch the carriages in the Park."

Mavis hesitated. The prospect of the sight of green trees, after the months spent within the four walls of the room, sounded very inviting, and already she pictured to herself the pleasure of escape, even for a moment, from the torture of her thoughts, for a new sight or sound to cheer her senses; but following quickly after was the dread of observation, of probable recognition. But in an instant it was checked by Dolores' rapturous exclamation of delight at the prospect.

"Do come; I'm sure it will do you a world of good—you look better already," urged her cousin, seconding the child's pleadings. "I will take great care of you; and you can sit down all the time, so as not to get tired against this evening."

And so Mavis yielded to the persuasions, and went into her bed-room to prepare for the expedition.

"Would it be possible for anybody to recognize me now?" she said to herself, as she stood before the glass, tying on her bonnet, and she almost smiled at the contrast in the pale, hollow cheeks and immense, mournful-looking blue eyes, to the radiant, exquisite beauty she had formerly possessed.

"It is only a faded caricature of my old self," she added. "I wonder what Lionel would say if he saw me now!" She turned hastily away, for her eyes were filling with tears, and the figure in the glass was getting blurred and indistinct, and her hands trembled as they tied a thick veil over her face. A few minutes after, leaning back in the corner seat in an omnibus, she was silently watching Dolores' delight at the sight of the crowded, gay thoroughfare, and enjoying, with the appreciation of one to whom pleasures are things of the past, the knowledge that her child was happy.

At length, leaning on Edward Austin's arm, she was walking slowly along in the sunshine, glancing up occasionally, not, however, without a secret pang of envy and regret, towards the well-dressed occupants of the carriages that were rolling past in quick succession. It appeared like a glimpse into the past, as if the dark mist that was closing round her, shutting out all that was bright or cheerful from her life, had suddenly rolled away, and for a moment she forgot all her miseries, all the wearied oppression of ill-health, as she looked around, scarcely realizing the wide gulf that lay between her and those happy beings who had formerly been her associates and equals.

But soon recollection came back, bringing with it the dreary blank of the present and future, with terrible vividness.

"Oh, Edward! I wish I had never come here," she cried. "I did not know, I never realized until now, how great the change has been in my life."

She sank back on a seat, covering her face to shut out the sight.

"Let us come away," she continued, "I cannot bear this."

The young man stared at her with undisguised astonishment.

"Why, Mavis, I thought you'd enjoy it," he said. "I never saw more carriages about in my life. Look there! that's a fine turn out: why, bless me, if there isn't young Durant!"

The mention of the name brought all the colour rushing back into Mavis's face. Involuntarily she looked up and rose to her feet, gazing in the direction that Edward indicated. Her eyes fell on the well-remembered features of Ivor Durant; he was seated in a carriage, drawn up close to where she stood; so near that she could hear his voice, as he bent forward to speak to a friend.

With a painful intensity, an almost feverish delirium that was urging her to prolong the agony produced by the sight of those who connected with her former life, she stood as if rooted to the spot, and her heart gave one great throb of mingled pain and surprise when she beheld his companion and recognized her cousin Jessie seated by his side, leaning back in the comfortable carriage. Mavis had not heard of Jessie's marriage with Ivor, and it was with astonishment that she beheld the girl, whom she had last seen in the country parsonage, elegantly dressed, in a style that instantly proclaimed to Mavis that a change had taken place in her cousin's fortunes.

The other occupant of the carriage was Sybil Montieth. Mavis only gave one glance into the face of her former friend, and then she heard Ivor's voice.

"How do you do, Hamilton?" he called out, and a gentleman passing in front of Mavis went up to the side of the carriage and shook hands cordially with Ivor and Sybil.

"I had no idea you had returned from Rome," he continued. "You surely have not forgotten your promise of paying us a visit at St. Hilda's."

"I arrived in London only last week," replied Louis Hamilton, for it was he. "I certainly have not forgotten my promise."

But Ivor resumed,—

"I must introduce you to my wife. Jessie, this is Mr. Hamilton; you have heard me speak of him."

This was all Mavis could hear, for several people were passing at the time between her and the carriage, from which she shrank back, as if in fear of recognition; but she saw Jessie's smile as she bent forward to greet her husband's friend, and then she watched him turn towards Sybil and enter into friendly conversation, until the carriage, following the stream of vehicles, was obliged to pass on, and Louis Hamilton raised his hat and turned away.

"Who are they?" she heard one of his friends inquire, as he again rejoined them.

"The Honourable Ivor Durant and his bride," was the reply. "I met him some years ago in Rome. He has not long been married; the other lady is the wife of an artist—Monteith, who has sent a picture to the Academy this year. I have made an appointment to meet them there in an hour's time and be introduced to Lord Durant."

"Lord Durant!" echoed the stranger. "I have heard of him. What has induced him to leave his hermitage? I thought he had given up his life to good works, or something of the sort!"

As he spoke they passed on out of Mavis's sight and hearing, but she had heard enough. "Lord Durant in London!" the words were ringing in her ears as she turned towards her cousin.

"Let us come away!" she said, faintly; "I do not want to be here if that carriage comes round again."

With a delicacy and consideration for her feelings for which Mavis would not have given him credit, Edward Austin made no attempt to break in on her thoughts, but, offering her his arm, he supported her feeble steps, walking slowly and silently along the crowded streets.

He could see how pale she had become, how her eyes shone with a feverish brightness, and he felt her leaning heavily on his arm, as if her strength had rapidly given way.

"Let me call a cab; you are not well enough to walk," he said at length, looking down into the face that seemed to have undergone a visible change in those few minutes.

"No, no!" exclaimed Mavis, with a vehemence that astonished him. "I feel much better, indeed I do. I can easily walk all the way home, the air revives me so much. Don't let us drive; it is not often I get out of doors."

With another puzzled and dissatisfied look into her face, Edward complied with her request.

"Remember that you have to sing this evening. Do not go and overtire yourself, because Bennett won't put up with excuses," he began, in remonstrance; but Mavis stopped him somewhat impatiently.

"I am all right, stronger than I have been for some time," she said. "I like to see the people passing; and Dolores would rather walk than ride."

"How happy young Durant looks with his wife! Upon my word it was a change for him!" exclaimed Edward, rather enviously, looking towards a passing carriage, after they had continued their way for some little distance.

Mavis had kept her eyes cast down all the while. She suddenly raised them on hearing her cousin's words.

Again Ivor Durant's carriage was passing swiftly by, and an irresistible fascination seemed to draw her gaze towards its occupants. She could almost feel the beating of her heart. An exclamation of mingled surprise and horror rose to her lips, for there, seated with his back to the horses, was Lord Durant!

He was looking her way, but there was a far off, wearied expression in his eyes, one of desolation and almost hopelessness, as if the joy had gone from his life. It was a momentary glimpse—a second after his face was shut out from her view—but it was enough, far more than sufficient to show the silvered hair, the altered expression, and bowed form, and to reveal to Mavis what she had done—how she had blighted his life.

She could not utter a word; it seemed as if a mist was closing round her senses. Her companion's eyes were turned the other way; he did not notice how the colour had fled from her face, how she was struggling for breath; her trembling limbs would scarcely support her, all the little strength she possessed had suddenly gone, but still she staggered onwards, clinging to Edward's arm. She heard the carriage draw up at a shop-door as if by instinct, for she could distinguish nothing; her only sensation was a longing to escape from Lord Durant's sight.

Then voices fell on her ear; they were strangely, painfully familiar.

"Look, Lord Durant, that woman must be ill."

It was Jessie who spoke, in gentle, low accents, that recalled time long past, with vivid distinctness.

The nobleman turned round sharply. He had descended from the carriage, and was assisting his daughter-in-law to alight: his penetrating gaze met Mavis's raised to his face with an agonized look of appeal. He made a step forward towards her; then, all at once, a thick, blank darkness came with overwhelming force, robbing her of consciousness, and she sank down at his feet.

Thrusting Edward Austin aside, Lord Durant raised her up in his arms; her bonnet had fallen off, and her bright, abundant hair fell over her in wreathing masses; she sank back pale and motionless, without a sign of life, but dazzlingly beautiful, with the fragile loveliness that even sorrow and hardship had been unable to destroy. Scarcely a moment had elapsed from the time she was lifted up before Mavis lay on a sofa in a room behind the shop, into which Lord Durant had carried her, and in speechless agony he bent over her senseless form. He did not utter a word, but Ivor and Jessie, who had followed him in, could understand the silent suffering; they could interpret his thoughts by the expression of his face. Even Edward Austin perceived it, and pitied him.

"Surely he must have loved Mavis," he said to himself, but it was time for action, not for thought, for the surgeon, who had been hastily summoned, had arrived.

"She is already dying," he declared, looking round at the group of bystanders. He spoke in a professional, unsympathetic tone, and then, whilst he was endeavouring with all the means in his power to restore the sufferer to consciousness, he was explaining to Lord Durant, with a coldness that seemed heartless, the nature of this sudden attack of illness, how heart-disease, probably augmented by trouble and privations of the necessaries of life, had brought this young life so early to an end. How could he tell what pain his words were causing to the nobleman? The faded-looking woman, dressed in shabby, threadbare garments, could be nothing to the aristocratic gentleman, whose demeanour alone, in the surgeon's eyes, proclaimed his high rank. And how should he know that the frightened, awe-stricken look on Jessie's face could be caused by any feelings but the mere sympathizing instinct of her sex, for one whose life was to all appearance already passing away? Ivor was the first to break the silence. With assumed indifference of manner he stepped forward.

"You must try and save her, poor young creature; do not hesitate: I will gladly defray any expenses."

"Indeed, my dear sir, it is very kind of you to say so," was the reply. "I shall certainly do my best to aid her, but I fear it is beyond my skill. We had better have her removed as soon as possible to the hospital."

All this time Edward Austin had remained silent, awed by the presence of Lord Durant. He felt powerless to act; he could only look on at the fruitless endeavours to restore Mavis to animation. Now, however, he came forward.

"My cousin shall not go to the hospital," he said, gruffly. "She has a home of her own, and there are friends who are able and willing to take care of her."

The surgeon looked scrutinizingly towards the speaker.

"I think you had better reconsider your wish," he said. "The young woman may linger on some days; she will have attendance and nursing at the hospital, far better than it could be at her home."

"No, no, she must be taken home; she will be taken care of there. Do you think I shall allow her to want for anything as long as I have strength to work? If everybody else deserts her I shall not do so; besides, there is a lady, a sister of mercy, who has always been very kind to her," exclaimed Edward, decisively.

A slight movement—a low moan from Mavis proclaimed that life was not yet extinct. Her bright eyes were fixed with a vacant look on the faces of the strangers who were in the room; she raised her thin, wasted hand, and tried to push back the thick, clustering hair from her forehead, but her strength failed,—it fell powerless by her side.

"Where is Dolores?" she asked, in a voice so faint that it surprised even herself. "What have they done with my child?"

Quietly Jessie led forward the wondering child, who could not understand what had happened to her mother; but all her merriment was subdued to gravity at the sight of the pale face.

With all her remaining strength Mavis half raised herself, and clasped Dolores to her heart in a close, clinging embrace, as if she feared to lose her from her sight. Again she felt the overpowering faintness stealing over her; it appeared as if everything was passing away; she still held the child with frantic dread, lest she too should vanish, until the low, frightened cries again recalled her scattered faculties.

It was almost more than Lord Durant could bear; his eyes were seeking hers, and yet he could not advance or utter a word. Struggling with his pity, his agonized regret, was a wild, passionate resentment against his brother who had brought her to this. He groaned and hid his face to shut out the sight of her terribly unconscious look, and the suffering visible in the restless eyes, so beautiful in their painful brightness.

"Ivor, please do not stay: take Jessie home," he whispered, hoarsely; "I will follow presently."

His son instantly obeyed him. The surgeon followed them from the room to give directions about his patient's removal, and Lord Durant and Edward Austin alone remained standing by Mavis's sofa.

The nobleman dropped on his knees by her side, and took one of the weak, helpless hands in his.

"Mavis, do you know me?" he asked, gently, gazing with pitying reverence into the half-closed eyes.

"Yes—Lionel," she murmured, the name coming faintly from her parted lips—"my love—"

With a start as if a serpent had stung him, Lord Durant flung away her hand and rose to his feet, an angry, lowering frown on his face. In that one moment his whole expression changed; the remembrance of the love that he had cherished, in spite of his struggles to put it from his heart, was passing rapidly away, and in its place was something approaching to aversion for the young creature whom he had formerly loved.

Fierce had been the love; the revulsion

that followed was fiercer still, and with the sound of his brother's name, as pronounced by her lips, still ringing in his ears, he turned and for ever left the presence of Mavis; passing through the shop, walking on aimlessly, not heeding in what direction he went, but, as if unconsciously, getting further away from the house in which Ivor had taken up his abode since the commencement of the London season.

He forgot all about his appointment at the Academy, for he had promised to go and see Claude Montieth's new picture. They waited for him in vain; his son expressed very little surprise at his non-appearance.

"We shall doubtless find that he has reached home before us," he said to the disappointed artist, for Claude had been looking forward to hearing the congratulations of his patron. "We had better return in time for dinner."

And so they left the Academy, and took their way to the home where Jessie reigned as mistress. She had already thrown off the constraint and diffidence that her quiet, secluded life had induced, and entered with all the zest of novelty into the pleasures and gaieties of her new life.

She was rather subdued and sad that evening. The unexpected meeting with Mavis had robbed her of some of her usual sprightliness; and she sat silent at the head of the dinner-table, only now and then joining in the conversation. It was not that the company was uncongenial to her tastes, for Ivor had invited one or two artist friends to meet Claude, and there was nothing Jessie liked much better than to talk of the art that her husband loved; but the absence of one whose face she was wont to see regarding her with fatherly tenderness caused her a pang of regret. She kept picturing to herself his grief, his desolation, at having his shattered love recalled as it had been that afternoon.

Dinner was nearly over when Lord Durant returned, rather paler and tired looking, but with very little trace of the violent emotion which he had struggled against and subdued.

To Ivor's observant eyes he seemed lighter hearted than usual, as if some heavy load had been taken from his mind. There was still the same gentle, benevolent expression in his eyes, but it was undimmed with the weight of care. And when all the visitors had gone, and he was preparing to retire for the night, and only Ivor and he stood alone in the room, he wrung his son's hand, with a look that spoke more than words.

"Ivor, I cannot feel regret now that her life is so nearly over," he said, in a low voice, one full of deep feeling; and in his heart (although he looked up with astonishment at hearing the words he had so little expected) Ivor could not gainsay them.

He knew now that the time for which he had been so long waiting had arrived, when he could reveal the fact of his mother's presence in London. The necessity for guarding her secret was over, and without hesitation, without pausing for consideration, he began relating the motives that had prompted Sister Veronica to her act of self-sacrifice in her care of Mavis. He went on eloquently, uttering the words that were uppermost in his mind; it seemed to him as if he were pleading his mother's cause, as if he would fain drive away the expression of resentment that Lord Durant's face had assumed at the first mention of his wife's name. At length Ivor paused. His father had kept silence all the time, listening to what he said, but making no reply. His head had been bent down in silent thought, but after a few minutes it was raised, and Ivor could see that the look of anger had disappeared.

"Poor Agatha!" he said, quietly, as he turned as if to leave the room. "Perhaps I have judged her harshly. She is indeed a good woman. I had no idea of this. Why did you not tell me before?"

"She wished it kept secret," replied Ivor. "Do you think she is one who would proclaim her good deeds to the world?"

Again there was silence, and Ivor still lingered. Lord Durant appeared about to speak, but checked the impulse.

"Ivor, you must tell her how grateful I am!" he exclaimed, at last, abruptly; but he was interrupted by his son.

"Will you not consent to see her yourself?" he asked, almost reproachfully.

"Perhaps I may," was the reply, "some other day—not just yet, for I could not bear it."

CHAPTER XIII.

PARTING.

He asked no question, all were answered now
By the first glance of that still marble brow;
It was enough—she died—what reck'd it how?
The only living thing he could not hate
Was reft at once—and he deserved his fate.
BYRON.

EVER since Isabel's departure for her visit to Mrs. Melcombe, which had extended over many months, Major Durant had remained at his mother's house. He saw no reason why he should leave. His wife was happier away from him. She wrote occasionally—cold, formal letters, in answer to his that were so few and far between. He openly declared that it was merely a sense of duty that caused him even to keep up a correspondence with her.

"It would be so annoying," he said, "for the people at St. Hilda's to suspect that Mrs. Durant could not agree with her husband; besides," he added, when alone with his mother, "I bear Isabel no ill will; it is as much my fault as hers. She prefers Mrs. Melcombe's society, and I am contented."

As time passed on he had begun to consider his mother's house as his own. The recollection of Mavis had almost faded from his mind, she had so completely passed from his sight, and had drifted away out of the world of music in which, for so short a period, she had shone with such brilliancy, and then sank down, unheeded and forgotten by the fickle public, into the unlovely, desolate existence that was so soon to come to an end.

Perhaps a few regretful thoughts of his lost love were lingering in his mind as he lay back lazily in his easy-chair, with the morning paper open before him. He had not yet finished his breakfast, although it was nearly twelve o'clock. He preferred to linger over the meal, until the time came to go out and see his friends. But on this particular morning he felt more than usually disinclined for exertion.

It was one of those chilly, damp spring mornings, with a cutting east wind that rendered it peculiarly uninviting out of doors, and caused the bright, cheerful fireside to be by far the most desirable. The previous day had been warm and fine—almost summer like—the contrast making the weather appear particularly disagreeable.

And as Major Durant yawned over his newspaper, complaining of the scarcity of news, and once or twice ringing the bell, startling the servant with angry, contradictory orders, his mother sat upright in her stiff-backed chair, composedly regarding him, whilst her fingers were busily employed with her knitting.

She did not seem in the least ruffled in temper. There was a sullen, heavy look of unemotional gravity about her whole bearing so different from the energetic vivacity by which her ambitious nature had formerly tried to triumph over any obstacles that presented themselves to her.

"I wish you would not speak in that way to the servants, Lionel; it causes them to be disrespectful," she said, presently, in a wearied, fretful tone.

"Then they ought to obey me!" he retorted; "but upon my honour I think I'm out of temper to-day. This confounded rain has upset all my plans."

"You should control your irritability," replied his mother. "Think what I have to endure, and what I have put up with cheerfully and uncomplainingly for your sake: you have even robbed me of my best friend, Mrs. Melcombe. I had looked forward to her companionship and sympathy as a solace in my old age, and even that consolation is gone, for as long as she upholds Isabel's conduct, how can I hope for a renewal of her friendship? Ah, as I have told you before, Lionel, I have sacrificed very much for you; you ought to feel grateful."

"And so I am grateful," replied the major, rather impatiently. "Have I not shown my gratitude by coming back to live here? Why what do you want now?"

The last words were addressed to a footman, who had entered the room.

"If you please, sir, you are wanted," he said. "A young man has called on urgent business. He is waiting in the library."

"A young man, you say—begging, I suppose. Tell him to send his name and his errand," spoke up Major Durant.

The man retreated, and soon returned, his face flushed with anger.

"He will give no message, sir. He declares he will not stir a step until he sees Major Durant, if he has to stay all day. He says his name is Austin."

"I suppose I must go and get rid of him," said the major, and his countenance fell a little at the mention of the name. It brought unpleasant thoughts into his mind, but his mother interrupted him.

"No, Lionel; if I were you, I would not pay any attention to such an impertinent message. Let Stevens or Dawes order him out of the house."

"Nonsense!" retorted her son. "He can do me no harm. If he wants money, I shall send him away quickly."

As he spoke he passed into the hall, and, entering the library, found himself face to face with Edward Austin. He did not recognize him, for he had never seen him before, but felt rather relieved in perceiving merely a shabby, common-looking stranger.

"What is your business with me?" he inquired, haughtily. "I suppose you want money: if so you have come to the wrong place. I never encourage idleness, especially in a strong, able-bodied fellow like you."

"Major Durant, I never asked a penny from you or yours," cried Edward, in a voice that vibrated with suppressed passion. "My errand is a far different one. I have come to bring your wickedness home to you, and tell you that soon, before this day is out, a death will lie at your door, and she, who but for you would have been happy and virtuous, is even now dying. Yesterday she was brought home insensible and suffering; and all through this winter she has been struggling with illness and want produced by your heartlessness."

Major Durant listened without interrupting the young man's angry speech. His heart smote him with reproach; he could not prevent a shudder of horror, although with an effort he attempted to assume calmness. "I do not know what you mean," he began. "To whom do you allude?"

"Ah, Major Durant! you know what I mean.; I can see it in your face. I am her cousin; I know her sad history," continued Edward Austin, in an altered tone of voice. "The news I bring has shocked you; you did not expect it—and no wonder. Poor Mavis! barely twenty-six years of age, and to die like this!"

There was silence for a few minutes. Major Durant had averted his face; he could not bear to meet the gaze even of one whom ten minutes before he would have regarded as so far beneath him in every respect. At length he looked up; a brighter, more hopeful look crossed his gloomy face. "Where does she live?" he asked.

Edward gave the required address, and then turned towards the door. "Do you wish to see her, sir?" he asked, more respectfully than he had before spoken. "Because there is no time to be lost. She cannot last long."

"The sooner I see her the better," was the major's reply. "I will accompany you."

Together they left the house. Major Durant hurried along by Edward's side, his brain in a strange whirl of excitement and emotion, that drove all thoughts from his mind except the knowledge that she, whom he had loved with all the ardour of his selfish heart, was dying. "What if she should be already dead! What if he should be too late to implore her forgiveness!" was the idea that hastened his pace, and he did not pause until he entered the room where Mavis was. One glance around was sufficient to reveal to him the evident poverty of her surroundings; but that was all; he did not perceive the tall, nun-like figure of Sister Veronica seated by the bedside, who rose when he came in. His eyes were riveted on Mavis's face, and he saw a look of recognition pass across it when his footfall reached her ear, and then came a smile, merely a fleeting expression, that emboldened him to advance.

"Mavis, my darling, my treasure! has it come to this?" he cried, in a voice that expressed the grief that again beholding her had caused, and flinging himself on his knees by the bedside, he tried to take one of the little wasted hands. "Speak to me! I cannot let you die like this. Say you forgive me!" he implored.

She did not attempt to withdraw her hand, but let it rest in his. Her lips moved as if she would try to speak. Deep agonized sobs of remorse choked his utterance; he could not have spoken a word, and for some minutes Mavis's weary eyes were content to regard him in silence. A few tears stole down her wasted cheeks. "Lionel," she murmured, presently. It was scarcely an utterance; the name was just breathed through her pallid lips, but he heard it, and rose to his feet and gazed down at her earnestly, with a long, eager look, as if he could not take his eyes from the features whose fragile loveliness was planting the sting of self-contrition deeper into his heart. There were tears in Sister Veronica's eyes also; she stood at the other side of the room unnoticed, watching the silent, sad parting, that to her mind spoke of deep sorrow and affection.

Dolores, seated on her mother's bed, was looking up with childish admiration into the major's face, her round eyes were gazing at him with awe-struck wonder, for even into her unformed mind the idea had just dawned that something terrible was happening to her mother. Presently, as with the last effort, Mavis raised her head and looked towards her child, she tried to speak, but her strength failed; however, the look was enough. "Yes, I will take her, Mavis," he said, solemnly. "It is my duty to provide for our child."

The words appeared to reassure her; a calmer, happier expression crossed her features, and with her eyes fixed on the face she loved, and her hand clasped in Lionel's, her life passed away.

The major's cry of distress at the change brought Sister Veronica to the bedside, and turning round, for the first time their eyes met.

"The troubled sinful life is over. Poor creature!" said Sister Veronica, calmly. "Lionel Durant, does your conscience hold you guiltless for this premature death? But for you, this poor girl (for she is little past her girlhood) might have been happy—beautiful and accomplished as she was—and look what a wreck lies here."

"Agatha," exclaimed Major Durant, addressing her by the name by which he had known her, "I do not need your reproaches. Have I not repented sufficiently already? Leave me alone just now; I cannot bear it."

She said no more, but drew back, and allowed Major Durant to press the one last kiss on Mavis's pallid brow, before he turned away to leave the room; his face had grown strangely haggard and wearied in the last few minutes.

"I will send for the child," he said, quietly; "and, Agatha, I have yet to ask your forgiveness."

"For what?" she asked, raising her eyes and surveying his troubled features.

"For the wrong I have done you. It was not my fault; duty to my mother demanded my silence."

"Do not seek to make excuses for your conduct, Lionel Durant. I despise you; I always did, and always shall. You had better go now; and may the hard trial you have endured to-day be of benefit to you."

She held the door open for him to pass through; and Major Durant, feeling subdued and humbled, passed out, with the reproaches that he knew he deserved still ringing in his ears.

CHAPTER XIV.

RECONCILIATION.

Time and tide had thus their sway,
Yielding, like an April day,
Smiling noon for sullen morrow,
Years of joy for hours of sorrow.
                                SCOTT.

SISTER VERONICA sat alone in her small dismal parlour. It was a rare thing to see her unoccupied, leaning back in an easy-chair, as she was then, with a languid expression, as if overcome by weariness of body and mind.

It was fast growing dark. She had been trying to read by the firelight; but her eyes were tired, and her head ached, so she allowed the book to lie open on her lap.

The work that she found so much harder

in London than in the more genial Italian climate was beginning to tell upon her health, but it did not altogether account for the look of melancholy depression. The painful scene of the last few days, Mavis's long illness and subsequent death, had produced an effect on her mind. The sad history was so painfully familiar to her and, accustomed as she was to suffering and sorrow, the whole occurrence had too close a connexion with her own life to pass unheeded.

"Mother!"

The exclamation caused her to start; so wrapped had she been in her own thoughts that she had not noticed Ivor's entrance, and, until he spoke, was unaware that he had come into the room.

She rose up, and, in her usual calm manner, greeted him cordially.

"I did not expect to see you," she said: "it is an unlooked-for pleasure. Have you brought your wife to see me?"

"No; Jessie has not come to-day," answered Ivor. "My errand is not one of pleasure, but a painful duty. My father is in London."

" In London!" ejaculated Sister Veronica, and the startled look that allusion to Lord Durant produced presently passed away.

"Yes; and he is anxious to see you. I could keep your secret no longer; there was no occasion for it, for his life-long grief is ended now," said Ivor.

" By the death of Mavis," continued his mother. " Yes, poor young creature! it is better for her—better for all of us—that the erring life is ended. Does he feel sorrow? Can he still think of her?"

" Do you blame him?" asked Ivor, for his mother's manner seemed cold and unsympathizing. " Remember how great his troubles have been."

"I do not blame him," replied Sister Veronica. "I am willing enough to forget and forgive the past, if he can forgive my conduct. I can see it now in its true light—how my selfishness has been the real cause of so much unhappiness, unintentional, it is true, but none the less blameworthy for that.

I never ought to have left my husband, when he needed my care and sympathy so much. I was cruel to allow my resentment to conquer my sense of duty; but ah, I was bitterly mistaken."

"By your last words I conclude that you are willing to see my father, now that he is desirous of an interview," said Ivor, presently. "For my sake, will you consent to it? I cannot bear to know that this estrangement exists between my parents."

He quietly waited for an answer, for he saw that various emotions were contending for mastery in his mother's heart. At length she spoke.

"It shall be as you wish," she said, averting her face.

In a moment Ivor had quitted the room. He presently returned, accompanied by Lord Durant; then turned away, and, closing the door, went downstairs, his heart filled with happiness at the prospect of the reunion that he had longed for so ardently.

The nobleman was the first to speak.

"Agatha, I would not intrude my presence on you," he began, "until I learned from our son that I should not be unwelcome. Is it too late now? After all we have passed through, will it not be better that all misunderstanding should cease. Can you forgive me?"

He was striving to assume calmness, but finding himself face to face with his wife, brought back too vividly the time when he had last seen her. Sister Veronica, however, preserved her usual quiet demeanour.

"Can you forgive my conduct in leaving you as I did?" she asked; "when I so completely forgot a wife's duties? But I was unfeeling; I never even allowed pity to enter my heart. Oh, Gerald! it is only your generosity that can make you forget the injuries I have done you. You think me cold and hard-hearted," she resumed. "I was so once: since that time I have passed through a bitter ordeal of repentance; I have tried to find rest to an accusing conscience by devoting myself to work, but it has been unavailing. Work—even the knowledge I am doing good, will not bring complete peace."

"Ah, but it does," was the reply. "I once felt as you do, Agatha. For years I gave myself up to selfish repinings—I knew no rest: now, at length, peace has come. Whilst *she* lived, and I knew my affection, though weakened, was not destroyed, what could I do? I have now learned that what has happened is all for the best." He paused, and for the first time met his wife's gaze: she read his thoughts as clearly as if they had been written.

"You want me to help you in your good work at St. Hilda's?" she said, interrogatively; and, covering her face, she burst into tears. "Am I worthy of it? Gerald, it cannot be so!"

"Not even for Ivor's sake?" asked the nobleman. "I am a lonely old man, Agatha; all these years of trouble have at least taught me forbearance; but perhaps I am asking too much."

"No, no! indeed I have the most need of repentance," she answered. "Since I have watched by the bedside, and seen the life which, but for my deception, might have been happy, ebbing slowly away, I have learned a new lesson; it showed my conduct in its proper light. It was for your sake, Gerald, that I devoted myself to her—to try and atone—"

She utterly broke down, and, covering her face, wept bitter tears of contrition; but there was no longer any opposition on her part. There were many mutual explanations to be gone through, and when at length Ivor returned, at his father's summons, he found the reunited husband and wife together, and a smile of content shone on his mother's face, increasing the calm beauty of expression that would never change in life.

And so they returned to the Abbey, and a new era dawned in Lord Durant's life. Their bitter experience had taught them both the duty of forbearance; they had the satisfaction of knowing that their names were mentioned with reverence by their poorer neighbours, amongst whom their life was spent. Maud still remained with her kind guardian; he would not part with her. Under the gentle influence of Sister Veronica (by which name the child was taught to call her) she grew to resemble her in mind and disposition, as in features she still retained the likeness to Mavis. '

And the day-dream that Ivor had scarcely dared to entertain in the days when the artist ambition had first been awakened, was at length realized. He and Jessie took up their abode at Pen Vychan Castle. The return to his native village was not, as he had once hoped, in the full triumph of a successful artist; but, raised to an eminence to which he had never dared to aspire, he settled down amongst the villagers whom he had known from childhood.

Of Major Durant his brother never heard. Isabel still remained at the Deanery; but Lionel had disappeared after Mavis's death, taking Dolores with him. He went to America, living only for the child, in whom the affection of his life seemed bound up. She could not return this affection, her mind was not capable of it; but she resembled her mother, and grew up even more lovely than Mavis had been, perfect in feature, but imbecile in mind.

The dowager Lady Durant, after her son's disappearance, sank down into a miserable old age, unloved and unlovely, and on her death-bed had not a single friend to mourn her loss: shunned even by her quondam friend, Mrs. Melcombe.

As time passed on, again the sound of children's voices was heard, awakening the echoes in the gloomy Abbey.

Ivor and Jessie had come on a visit to St. Hilda's, bringing with them their two children. There was no longer any fear in Lord Durant's mind as he watched his little grandson and future heir at play beneath the shade of the old trees.

Perchance his thoughts wandered to the other little Mervyn, who lay in the vault beneath the old cathedral; but the curse had gone from the family; the past had been outlived, and peace and content reigned in its place.

THE END.

LONDON:
PRINTED BY E. J. FRANCIS AND CO.,
TOOK'S COURT AND WINE OFFICE COURT, E.C.

www.ingramcontent.com/pod-product-compliance
Lightning Source LLC
Chambersburg PA
CBHW031931230426
43672CB00010B/1890